MY SECOND BEDTIME BOOK OF

Two-Minute Stories

EDITED BY MARY PARSLEY

Illustrated by Tony Escott

Peter Lowe

Original title: Daddy, read me a bedtime story.

ISBN 0 85654 045 5

Printed in Spain by Graficas Reunidas

Introduction

This book contains 42 short stories for young children—but is written with parents very much in mind. The stories are all just the right length for reading aloud at bedtime and are perfect for those few quiet moments during the day as well.

Each story takes just two minutes to read aloud and is illustrated in colour with delightfully humorous paintings by cartoonist and illustrator Tony Escott. The subjects include adventurous animals, eccentric inventors, magicians, ships, trains, cars and, of course, children themselves.

Bedtime stories are for sharing and it's much nicer for everyone if the grown-ups enjoy what they are reading as well as the children. That's why the stories and pictures in MY SECOND BEDTIME BOOK OF TWO-MINUTE STORIES *are always fun—and often funny—even for grown-ups!*

Make reading a bedtime story to your children a daily habit. The whole family will enjoy it!

List of Stories

Sports Day at the Zoo

It was Sports Day at the Zoo. All the animals wore running vests. Each had a large number on his vest. The Lion had a big vest and his number could be seen for miles. The Centipede's vest was much smaller: his number was rather hard to see.

The first race began. It was a Running Race. Major Bark, who owned the Zoo, gave the signal. The Hyena howled, the Monkey fell over, and the Antelope won the race.

The second race was a Flying Race. The winner was the Swift. The Emu was most upset when Major Bark told him he could not take part.

"But I'm a bird," wailed the Emu. "And even if I haven't got real wings, I'm jolly fast on land."

"Quite, quite," said Major Bark. And he gave the Emu a special prize for being the Fastest Bird Unable to Fly.

The third event was a Diving Contest. This was won by the Seal. His dive was not so beautiful as the dive of the Salmon, but the Seal earned extra marks for staying underwater for over an hour. The Giraffe won the High Eating Contest with a magnificent nibble of nineteen feet. The Animal Cunning Prize went to the Chimpanzee. He locked all his rivals in the changing-room.

Then it was time for the Grand Obstacle Race. All the earlier winners took part. They were the Swift, the Antelope, the Emu, the Seal, the Giraffe and the Chimpanzee.

From the start the animals had to run or fly to a low wall and climb over it. Then they had to wriggle under a fishing net by the fish pool. After that there was a short swim across the fish pool, and then a final race to the finishing line.

The Swift was easily first over the low wall, but he caught a wing in the fishing net and was stuck. The Antelope had his best horns on, and one of these, also, became jammed in the fishing net. The Emu was so

excited about the race that he kept tripping over. In the end he had to be helped to a chair by Major Bark. That was the Emu out of the race.

The Seal puffed and blew and was left far behind by the other animals. The Giraffe set off smartly, then he slowed down.

"I don't know what's wrong with me," said the Giraffe to Major Bark. "But I can't seem to run very fast."

"That," said Major Bark, "is because the Chimpanzee is riding on your back." Then Major Bark gave the Chimpanzee a Severe Warning and sent him back to the Start.

A few moments later the Giraffe, too, with his great long neck, was stuck in the fishing net, together with the Swift and the Antelope. Then the Chimpanzee caught all the others. He wriggled easily under the net and came to the fish pool. The Chimpanzee was in the lead. But he could not swim.

The fishing net was no problem to the Seal, either, when he finally reached it.

"I'm so smooth, I'm so smooth," he gloated to the other animals who were stuck there. And he flopped away to the fish pool. There he met the Chimpanzee.

"Look," said the Chimpanzee, "we're the only two left in the race. But I can't swim. Wouldn't it be much more sporting if you gave me a lift to the other side of the water. Then I'll give you half a minute's start to the finishing line."

"All right," said the Seal. "Hop on."

The Chimpanzee clung to the Seal's shiny neck and they started off together. But the Seal's back was so slippery that the Chimpanzee kept sliding off.

"Watch out!" cried the Chimpanzee to the Seal. "I keep sliding off your back."

"How nasty for you, old boy," said the Seal. "I think I'd better drop you off on this little island." And he flipped the Chimpanzee onto a small rocky island halfway across the fish pool. The Chimpanzee was furious and danced up and down with rage.

Then the Seal swam to the other side, and waddled up to the finishing line. He was declared the winner by Major Bark, and everyone clapped and cheered.

"How shiny and beautiful you are," said Mrs. Major Bark to the Seal, as she gave him his prize.

"Thank you, ma'am," said the Seal. "I'm fairly slippery, too."

The Magic Sheep

Once, in Wales, there was a magic sheep who could jump higher than any of his other brothers and sisters. The farmer who owned the sheep found that however high he built fences around the field where the sheep were grazing, this one would always jump over it and come to the kitchen door. When the sheep saw the farmer it would jump over the kitchen table to try to get away from him.

Very often it knocked over the butter churn which stood on the table, and its wool would be full of milk and butter. One day when this happened the farmer got so angry that he got out his sheep shears, although it was not sheepshearing time, and cut all the wool off the poor sheep.

"That'll teach you to jump all over the kitchen," he said. The sheep started to feel cold and sorry for itself.

The farmer gathered up all the buttery and milky wool and put it in a pile on the kitchen table. He then stumped off to bed and told his wife that there was some wool in the kitchen if she wanted to knit anything.

During the night something funny happened to the mixture of butter and milk and wool on the table. There were lots of grunts and chuckles coming from it, and in the morning all the butter had disappeared, and so had all the milk.

"Hey ho," said the farmer's wife as she got up to milk the cows early in the morning. She came thumping down the stairs in her gumboots, which she only took off when she went to bed.

"Daisy! Milly! Parsley! Wocky!" she called and all the cows started to come in from the fields to be milked. The cows were never any trouble to the farmers. The farmer's wife started to walk outside to milk the cows who were lining up in the yard, when she fell flat on her face in front of all of them. "Daisy! Milly! Parsley!–" SPLAT! she tripped over the wool which had somehow threaded itself into a long string and wrapped itself round two milk churns. The milk churns rolled down the hill, and the cows looked away politely.

The farmer's wife got up and went upstairs to the farmer, who was still asleep. She took off her gumboot and hit him on the head with it. "That's what you get for setting traps for me like that," she said and stumped downstairs again. The farmer was a very heavy sleeper and didn't even wake.

It wasn't the farmer who had tripped his wife up. It was the wool.

Later in the day the farmer's wife picked up the long strand of wool and started to darn a hole in one of the farmer's socks with it. She didn't know that it was the wool which the farmer had cut off the sheep in big tufts the night before. Whatever she did the wool seemed to come undone of its own accord. She had to hold one end in her teeth while she darned with the other end, to stop it untying itself.

The farmer was very pleased that the wool had been put to good use. The next morning he put his socks on much earlier than usual and ran downstairs to help his wife with the milking.

It was very strange. One foot seemed much lighter than the other. The foot that wore the darned sock was trying to rise. Woops! He sat down and the foot immediately rose in front of him. It was getting worse. He shouted for his wife to come and help.

"Take the sock off, or I'll fly straight up in the air in a minute!" he shouted. His wife

left the cows and ran to sit on his leg to stop it rising up. But soon, even her weight was not enough.

"Take my boot off," the farmer shouted "and let the sock fly off if it wants to!" The farmer's wife took his gumboots off with a great struggle and tugged at the sock.

Whoosh! It flew straight up in the air and made off towards the field of sheep.

"Catch it! There's a good sock there!" shouted the farmer. When they reached the field, there was no sign of the sock, but the magic sheep had got its coat back.

"It must be magic," said the farmer's wife.

The sheep, behind the farmer's back, smiled and did a tiny little jump.

Stanley Finds a Home

Stanley was a scarecrow. He stood in Farmer Furrow's largest field and kept the birds away from the young seeds. He was very elegantly dressed. He wore an old top-hat left over from Farmer Furrow's wedding, a dog-tooth check jacket and plain brown trousers. His gloves and scarf had holes, but were nicely knitted. He was smart enough to stand in the proudest farmer's field.

Stanley had many friends living nearby. Even the fastest-moving animals, the rabbits and the hares, slowed down to pass the time of day with him. The field-mice and the hedgehogs, having more time to spare, stayed to chat with him when he was not too busy scaring the birds. But strangely enough, Stanley's best friend was a bird. The bird's name was Indigo, and he was a bluebird. Indigo was the only bluebird in the neighbourhood. No one knew where he came from. The other, more ordinary birds, the crows, starlings and rooks, were not very friendly with the blue stranger, and Indigo thought they were too noisy to have as neighbours. So he had made his home in the place where he knew they would not come – in Stanley's pocket! He had asked Stanley's permission first and Stanley, being kind-hearted, had agreed, provided that Indigo did not steal too many seeds or leave any worms in his pocket. They soon became great friends.

All through spring and summer Stanley stood guard in his field. At harvest time the crop in Stanley's field was especially fine, so Farmer Furrow decided to leave him there ready to do another good job next year. He padded Stanley out with some new stuffing where he had become floppy, and tied on his gloves more firmly.

The weather grew colder. Indigo snuggled warmly in Stanley's pocket, and the other birds tucked their heads under their wings and hoped that the winter would not be too hard. But poor Stanley stood and shivered.

"I'm so cold," he said to Indigo, who looked up at him from his pocket. "When evening comes, all the birds and animals are snug in their nests and holes, and Farmer Furrow warms himself by his fire. But I have to stand here with the wind snatching at my stuffing and the frost pinching my finger-tips through the holes in my gloves."

"Oh dear," said Indigo, sympathetically. "But you cannot climb a tree and build a nest, and you're too big to creep into a burrow. Where do scarecrows live in winter?"

Neither of them had any idea, so poor Stanley kept on shivering at night and hated the thought of snow.

One day, they saw Farmer Furrow plodding across the field, followed by two strangers.

"Don't go too close," one of the men whispered. "We don't want to scare the bluebird away."

"No, indeed," said the other man. "It's a very unusual bird that you have in your field, Farmer Furrow."

"Well, I must get back to work anyway,"

said the farmer. "You have my permission to build your hide anywhere you wish."

The two strange men at once began to collect leaves, grass and branches. After a while, they had built a little hut, into which they crawled.

"Whatever are they doing?" asked Stanley in amazement.

"I know," said Indigo. "They are bird-watchers, and they have built a hide. They sit inside and study birds through binoculars. They've come to watch me. I told you I was a most uncommon bird."

Indigo did not want to be watched all the time, but he was prepared to put up with it because he had an idea.

"Stanley!" he exclaimed. "There's the perfect home for you – in the hide! The men go away at night!"

Stanley was delighted by the plan. So all through the winter, he spent the cold nights tucked up in a corner of the hide, with Indigo in his pocket. And thanks to his friend, he didn't feel chilly at all.

The Lobster Who Knew Everything

Baldwin was a clever lobster who lived on a steep black rock in the Far North where the sea is cold and there is not very much to do. Because there was not very much to do, Baldwin would spend all his time reading.

"If I can read all the books in the Far North, then I shall not only be a clever lobster but a superior one as well, and the shrimps will be truly afraid of me," he used to say to himself as he settled down with a book in the wavy brown seaweed.

One day his cousin, who was a very small shrimp, came to see him. Now small shrimps are not only very talkative but they tend to ask a lot of questions.

"Hello Baldy, what are you doing down here reading?" said the shrimp. The sea was very rough at the time and the shrimp, whose name was Morris, had to shout to make himself heard.

"Go away, I'm reading," said Baldwin. "And before you come back, my name is not Baldy, it is 'Mr. Baldwin Sir' to someone as small as yourself." Baldwin always talked as if he was the most important thing in the sea. But the shrimp was not listening.

"Don't you find it difficult when you have to turn the pages with those clumsy great claws?" Baldwin did not say anything at all, as it was very true. He tried to turn his back as he turned the page of the book. "Isn't it a mistake to read underwater? Isn't it bad for the eyes?" Morris the shrimp was in a good mood for annoying lobsters.

"If you want me to talk to you then you must start each sentence with *Mr. Baldwin Sir*," said Baldwin.

"Mr. Baldwin Sir, why?" said Morris, who did not mind this in the least.

"You have a squeaky voice," said Baldwin. "I can't tell if you are talking or someone has trodden on one of your feelers. Now what was the question that you asked?"

"Mr. Baldwin Sir, why?" said Morris, now rather frightened by Baldwin who had suddenly spoken loudly and appeared to grow larger at the same time.

"Why what?" said Baldwin, who had finished one book and picked up another.

Morris had forgotten what he was going to ask and so he remained quiet and swirled small patterns in the sand with his tail while the lobster, who was a fast reader, tore through three more books. Finally Baldwin sat back with a sigh.

"There," he said, with a lobsterish smile. "I have now read everything that has ever been written."

"Everything?" squeaked Morris.

"Call me *Mr. Baldwin Sir*," said Baldwin, "you cheeky little shrimp!"

Morris, although a small shrimp and one who had not read anything at all, decided that the lobster had been rude to him and that he must do something quickly to Baldwin or the lobster would never bother to speak to a shrimp again.

"Mr. Baldwin Sir. Can I ask a question?" said Morris.

"You may," said Baldwin proudly.

"Do you know *Everything* now?" asked Morris.

"Everything," said Baldwin. "Ask me any question, from the sausage tax in Normandy to the latest ways of making chewing gum out of old oil tankers, and I will tell you."

"Can I ask you three questions?"

"You *may* ask me three questions," said Baldwin. "And if I get even one wrong,

which is impossible, I shall allow you to call me Baldy as many times as you like."

The shrimp smiled. "What is the cause of storms?"

"Waves," said Baldwin crossly. "Ask me another."

"What causes waves?" asked Morris.

"Weather," said Baldwin. "Terribly easy, this – I know *Everything*."

"What," said the shrimp with his last question, "is my *name*?"

Baldwin had never bothered to learn anyone's name. "Cheeky little shrimp!" he shouted and chased Morris all around the steep black rock. But all the other shrimps knew that Baldwin had lost, and from that day on, they always called him Baldy.

Mr. Rabbit Builds a Nursery

Rabbits usually have large families. In May, Mr. and Mrs. Robert Rabbit had five new babies. They were noisy bunnies, who disturbed their older brothers and sisters.

"We must have a proper nursery for our new babies," said Mrs. Robert Rabbit. "Our burrow is so crowded now, and besides, the babies will need somewhere to play when the weather is bad."

"Well, it must not be too close to our sittingroom," answered her husband. "I need peace and quiet after a hard day's work. I'll dig out a passageway and build the nursery at the end of it. I'll begin first thing next Saturday morning."

On Saturday, Mr. Rabbit pulled on his oldest blue overalls. They had two coloured patches on each knee, and Mrs. Rabbit really wanted to throw them away, but Mr. Rabbit was fond of them. At half-past nine, their neighbour, Mr. Mole, knocked at the door. He was going to help Mr. Rabbit with his work. Mrs. Rabbit privately thought that Mr. Mole was silly to wear a velvet jacket for dirty work, but he had no other clothes.

"We'll begin at once," decided Mr. Rabbit, and called all his older children to help.

"We'd better dig over in that direction," he said, pointing to the left, "because we decided to make our winter storeroom on this side."

All five baby rabbits stared as Mr. Rabbit, Mr. Mole and the six older rabbit children started digging. The rabbits scrabbled and thumped with their paws, and Mr. Mole pushed with his strong snout. Soon they made an enormous pile of earth for Mrs. Rabbit to sweep outside.

After an hour, all the workers stopped for a refreshing mug of cocoa and biscuits.

Mr. Rabbit thought that the tunnel was now long enough and it was time to hollow out a larger space for the nursery.

Dusting themselves, the rabbits and Mr. Mole got ready to go on with their work. Puff! Pant! Scratch! What an effort!

Mr. Rabbit headed the team and encouraged his helpers.

"Come along – put your backs into it! Oh! Oh dear! Help!"

There was a tremendous crash and a shout. Mr. Rabbit suddenly disappeared.

Then came a cry.

"Oh Moley! Our wall has fallen in!"

Poor Mr. Rabbit had been digging in the wrong direction. He had made a huge hole

right into the wall of Mr. Mole's house next door. He had tumbled through into the Mole's kitchen and frightened Mrs. Mole so much that she had dropped a lovely saucepan of stew that she was cooking for lunch.

"I simply can't understand how I made such a silly mistake," moaned Mr. Rabbit, rubbing his back. He had landed very heavily, and was rather sore.

"And fancy you not noticing, Moley!" said Mrs. Mole crossly to her husband. "Now we've got an enormous hole in our kitchen wall and dirt all over my clean floor. And we've got no dinner – and it was your favourite!"

All the older rabbit children were peering through the hole into the kitchen, with their noses twitching in excitement. Some of them were giggling at the sight of their father, still tumbled in the heap of dirt. Back in her own kitchen, Mrs. Rabbit had heard all the commotion and rushed up the new tunnel to find out what had happened.

She was a practical creature. After she had comforted Mrs. Mole and invited her to dinner at her house, she organized her family. Two of the older children had to clean up Mrs. Mole's floor and the other four had to block up the tunnel again. And Mr. Rabbit had to go and have a hot bath.

It was late at night before the work was finished. While she was putting her babies to bed, Mrs. Rabbit thought that they would probably be grown up before Mr. Rabbit was ready to have another try at building a nursery.

The Day It Snowed

The snow started to fall so gently and slowly at first that no one noticed it. Not George sitting in the back of the car reading; not his sister Susan in the front doing a jigsaw puzzle; not Mother sitting in the back holding baby Lucy. Father, who was driving, noticed it of course. And so did all the others when the wind began to blow harder and flurries of snowflakes beat against the windscreen. Everyone got very excited.

"Isn't it fun having snow for the Christmas holidays!" Susan said.

"Not if we have too much of it, it won't be," Father interrupted. "We still have a long way to drive today." He was right, too, for soon even with the car lights on bright, they could see only a few inches ahead, and it was impossible to see the sides of the road.

Suddenly, with a bump and a soft thud, the car stopped dead. Without realizing it Father had driven off the road, and had hit a tree stump hidden under the thick snow.

They were completely stuck.

George and Susan thought it was terribly exciting, but Mother and Father were very worried.

"Whatever can we do?" Mother asked.

"Stay right where we are and wait for a snowplough to clear the road," Father replied. "The worst thing we can do is leave the car."

"That's all very well," Mother went on, "but what about milk for Lucy? I've got plenty of her dried milk, but I need hot water to mix with it for her to drink. I've enough ready-mixed to last until morning, but that's all!"

"Well, we've got to stay here for now," George said. "It's getting dark."

"And in the morning," Father said, "if no one comes to rescue us, then we'll just have to rescue ourselves – somehow."

So, all through the night they sat in the car, their teeth chattering with the cold, while the snow piled up round them. By the morning the car was almost buried.

They waited and waited. But still no snowplough came. Then, when there was just one feed of milk left for baby Lucy, Father decided to fetch help.

But things turned out differently, for he had hardly got out of the car before he fell in the snow and hurt his ankle.

So George and Susan went instead.

They took all the clothes out of their suitcases and put on as many as they could – high rubber boots, two pairs of socks, two pairs of trousers, lots of sweaters, gloves and scarves and coats and hats (George didn't have one, but wore one of Mother's – anything to keep warm).

They went as fast as they could. But the snow made it very difficult. It was deep everywhere, but in some places it had piled up very high, in some it was frozen and slippery, and in others, where there was a ditch or a hollow, it was much deeper than it looked.

George and Susan were tied together with the car tow-rope. They needed this rope, because first one then the other fell into deep snowdrifts and had to be pulled out.

"Look!" George shouted. "A house!"

They struggled to it and rang and rang the bell. The man who opened the door was very surprised.

"Good gracious!" he said. "Where did you come from?"

"Please, our car's stuck in the snow . . ." George began. "We've been there all night with our mother and father . . ."

". . . and our baby sister Lucy," interrupted Susan. "They've got nothing to eat, and Father's hurt his foot . . ."

". . . AND PLEASE HAVE YOU GOT A TELEPHONE?" both children said together.

After that things moved quite quickly. The man *did* have a telephone, and while George and Susan were having a hot drink he called the nearest village. A snowplough was soon on the way to rescue Mother and Father and Lucy.

"What an adventure!" George said, when they were all safely together again. "Just like something out of a book!"

"Yes, it was," said Susan, "but I think its nicer to read about. That way you don't get so cold."

Funny Friday

Mrs. Wedge, the daily help, shook with rage right from her three double chins down to her large carpet-slippered feet. She considered that she was being "put upon". She usually spent Friday afternoon sitting comfortably in the kitchen cleaning the silver, and here was this stuck-up little Miss Pugsey telling her that the parlour was a disgrace and must be dusted again at once.

Mrs. Wedge wheezed and muttered and scowled: she banged her mop in the bucket, she took it out again and shook it, but it was no good. Little Miss Pugsey stood firm. She just glared at Mrs. Wedge through her steel-rimmed glasses and pointed sternly to the parlour door.

At last Mrs. Wedge, with a furious snort, stamped off and soon began banging at all the furniture within reach of her angry mop.

"Gurcher," she snarled as she jabbed her mop under the sofa, and immediately there was a strange noise, something between a hiss and a squeak.

"Mice, the little devils," muttered Mrs. Wedge, who hated all animals. "I'll teach 'em," and she jabbed her mop in again. This was unfortunate for her because it was no mouse that she was disturbing, but Gumbo the Gremlin. Now gremlins are funny little creatures who live in odd corners in most houses. They are very small and they have bodies like putty which they can alter to any kind of shape. Although they often sleep for years on end, if they are disturbed they can turn quite nasty. This one did, for he changed himself into a sort of small octopus and quickly pulled one of Mrs. Wedge's feet from under her. With a bellow of rage she capsized into the nearest chair which collapsed under her weight. The noise was heard by Miss Pugsey who came bustling in to find out what was happening. Mrs. Wedge struggled to her feet and started to tell her, but Gumbo again seized her ankle and, grasping wildly for support, she flung her arms round Miss Pugsey and bore her heavily to the ground.

"Have you gone mad, Mrs. Wedge?" spluttered Miss Pugsey as she struggled painfully to her feet.

Mrs. Wedge was opening her large mouth to tell her, when exactly the same thing happened again, and the two furious women were once more rolling on the floor.

After this had happened three times, Miss Pugsey crawled out on all-fours leaving Mrs. Wedge to lever herself up as best she could.

Eventually both women reached what they imagined was the safety of the kitchen, and, in an attempt to soothe her nerves,

Mrs. Wedge made a cup of tea and tried to explain what had happened.

"It must be one of them nasties out of a zoo," she exclaimed.

"Zoo, my good woman, what nonsense! There's no zoo for miles around here."

"Maybe or maybe not," observed Mrs. Wedge heavily as she held out a cup with shaking hand, but the rest of her remark was lost as Gumbo jogged her elbow and all the tea spilled over into Miss Pugsey's lap.

"You clumsy idiot!" screamed Miss Pugsey. "I believe you're drunk!" and, grabbing the other cup of tea, she poured it all over Mrs. Wedge's head. A fight now seemed certain, but just at this moment both women noticed a strong smell of burning. Forgetting their differences, they rushed back to the parlour. Yes, the chimney was on fire. Mrs. Wedge had displaced so much in her struggles that the fender was full of blazing wreckage.

Far up in the sky the Salamanders were circling. These are great fiery lizards who live on the stars. But every hundred years they are driven by a strange urge to fly to the earth and lay their eggs there. They prefer volcanoes, of course, but a chimney on fire will do almost as well. (Besides, it is great fun, trying to drop an egg, plop, down a chimney.) If the egg does go down the chimney it hatches out right away, and the salamander either flies off to the stars or stays on earth and becomes something like a Loch Ness Monster. The Salamanders swooped down lower and lower.

"On target there; bombs away, Martha!" shouted one of them, and down came a salamander's egg, down, down, straight down Miss Pugsey's chimney.

"Bull's eye!" shouted a salamander, and they all started to do victory-rolls, which made lots of people ring up the police to report Flying Saucers.

At Miss Pugsey's there was considerable uproar and confusion. Mrs. Wedge was shouting out the window:

"Murder . . . police . . . help!"

Miss Pugsey was trying to telephone the Fire Brigade who were trying to telephone her.

The newly-hatched salamander was capering around the parlour, piling furniture on the fire and singing in a rather unmusical voice some song about reaching for the sky.

Gumbo the Gremlin slid away quietly through a convenient keyhole.

"And now for a little peace and quiet again," he murmured. "Where's my address book?"

Wozzo's Wand

Wozzo the wizard was very upset. He had hired a new servant, whom he asked to light the fire, and the servant had burned Wozzo's wand. He said he had thought that the wand was just an old stick, and by the time Wozzo realized that his wand was missing, it had been burned to a cinder.

Wozzo was only a beginner wizard, so he could not perform any magic, not even the simplest spell, without his wand. And to make things worse, today was the day that he was "At Home" to people who needed magic, and he had no time to go to the Wizard's Stores for a new wand. He tried a few spells, saying all the right words, and making all the right gestures with his fingers, but it was no good. Without his wand, his magic would not work. Whatever was he to do?

At that very moment, his first customer knocked at the door. It was an old man.

"Good morning, Wozzo," he said. "I've come to ask you to do some magic. The problem is that my beard keeps getting into terrible tangles with my coat-buttons whenever there is a strong wind. I want you to magic away my beard."

"Oh, dear!" said Wozzo. "I'm afraid I can't help you. My wand has been done for and I have no magic."

"No magic!" shouted the old man, crossly. "And you call yourself a wizard! Good day!" and he stamped off along the path.

"Toodleloo!" the wizard's parrot called.

A young girl was just arriving.

"Good morning, Wozzo," she said. "I need a spell. My little kitten has climbed up that tall tree near your gate and he can't get down. Will you cast a spell to make the tree bend over so that he can jump down?"

"Oh, dear!" said Wozzo. "I'm afraid I can't help you. My wand has been done for and I have no magic."

"No magic?" said the girl. "What about my poor kitten?" and she ran sobbing up the path.

"Toodleloo!" the wizard's parrot called.

Wozzo's next visitor was a little boy.

"Good morning, Wozzo," he said. "Do you remember that you said you would come to my party this afternoon and do some magic for us after tea?"

"Oh, dear!" said Wozzo. "I'm afraid I can't help you. My wand has been done for, and I have no magic."

"No magic!" exclaimed the little boy. "But my party will be spoiled!" and he went sadly away.

"Toodleloo!" the wizard's parrot called.

"I wish you'd stop saying that silly word," said Wozzo. "Here I am with no wand, and without a wand I've no magic, and without magic I can't do my job, and if I can't do my job we'll have no money, and with no money we'll have no food and we'll both starve. And all you can do is say toodleloo."

"I hadn't thought of it like that," apologized the parrot. "I'll think of a way to help. I don't want to starve."

So he sat on his perch and closed his eyes in thought.

After a few minutes, he beckoned to Wozzo.

"I've had an idea. Use my perch!"

"What do you mean – use your perch? If I want to sit down, I'll use a chair."

"Not to sit on, silly – use my perch as a wand. Its wooden, and just about the same size. As for me, well, it's a nice sunny day, so I can sit up in that tree."

"The very thing!" cried Wozzo, and undid the cage. He took out the wooden perch, and away flew the parrot, right up into the tall tree by the gate, where the kitten was. The kitten was so startled that he ran down at once, right into the young girl's arms.

"Oh, thank you, Wozzo!" she cried. "You did it after all."

The parrot cackled with laughter, and watched Wozzo try out his wand. It worked! Then Wozzo remembered what he had been asked, and the old man suddenly found himself without a beard.

"An even better trick now," said Wozzo, and touching an old twig with his wand, he said a few magic words and turned the old twig into a lovely new parrot's perch.

"You can come down now," he called to the parrot. "We've got a birthday party to go to," and off they went down the path.

"Toodleloo!" called out the parrot.

The Old Rat's Tale

"Grandpa, why do you like eating buttons?" Grandpa Gillie looked around at the eager faces of the little gormrats and then he cleared his throat:

"It is time, my children, that I told you the story of what you are. You all know that you are larger and cleverer than other rats?"

"Oh, yes!" chorused the little gormrats.

"You realize that you can balance easily on your back legs without falling over?"

Several little gormrats tried to do this and fell over.

"You know, too, that you are justly famous for your singing?"

The little gormrats broke at once into song, and it was some time before Gillie could proceed.

"Well, we could not always sing like this, but there was a great and noble man called Hermogenes Gorm who first showed us how to use this great gift."

"Was his name really Hermogenes?" squeaked the smallest gormrat and started to giggle. He was quickly cuffed into silence.

"Mr. Gorm," continued Gillie, looking around severely, "saw what splendid Pop singers we would make and he trained all the earliest and most famous gormrat groups: The Sniffers, The Cockchafers and the unforgettable Rollaround Rats."

All the little gormrats broke into loud cheering, which lasted for some minutes.

"We now became rich and famous," continued Gillie, "for in the Top of the Pops charts, nine of the top ten were written and sung by gormrats."

"And than a dreadful thing happened: men became jealous of us. Why should these gormrats be the Top of the Pops, they said. Why should thay have all the best disc jockeys?"

"They made a wicked plan. They would put our own Mr. Gorm in prison, and then he would not be able to train us any more. The dreadful thing was done, and many of us, just broken-hearted, disappeared into the shelter of our holes."

All the little gormrats groaned.

"But," cried out Gillie in ringing tones, "they had reckoned without ME! One night, with a few devoted helpers, I entered the prison when everyone was asleep. Now, you must not think that with all our singing we had forgotten how to use our fine, sharp teeth. Oh, no. We chewed up every single

button on every police uniform: shirts, tunics, trousers, the lot. Then we led our poor, dear Mr. Gorm to safety. Pursuit indeed was quite impossible, because all the policemen had to hold up their trousers as they ran. They could not even shake a fist at us."

The little gormrats cheered and stamped their feet in delight.

"After that," concluded Gillie solemnly, "we were friends with men no more, and we proudly called ourselves gormrats after our great singing master. And that is why every true gormrat enjoys eating a nice plate of buttons, to remind ourselves of our great rescue. So now, let us sing together our own special song. He led off in a fine nasal tenor:

"Gormrats of the world unite
You who love a good old fight.
Trim your whiskers, swish your tails,
Sing the song that never fails:
    Nip and nibble
    Munch and gribble,
Heart of gormrat never quails!"

"How do you gribble, grandpa?" asked a very small gormrat.

"That will be enough for this evening," replied the old gormrat. "It is time you were all in bed."

The Piggy-bank Thief

Bill Boffin was a really horrid man. He was fat, smelly and greedy, and he often stole money from children's piggy-banks. He did this because he thought that this was safer than stealing valuable stuff. He pretended he came from the gas company to check that the cookers were all right. Every Saturday he used to spend all his stolen money on vast quantities of his favourite food – fried fish and chocolate marshmallows.

Well, one Friday afternoon Boffin had had a successful day. Just one more job, he thought, and then I'm for home. His mouth began to water at the thought of all that fish and marshmallows he would guzzle the next day. He pressed the bell of a quiet looking house and stood feeling very pleased with himself. All his stolen money lay safe in a large bag he carried. He pretended it was full of tools.

When the door opened he thought that the lady looked at him rather hard and so he decided that he would be as quick as possible on this job. So quick indeed that he caught his trousers on a nail. He said a very rude word, but the nail didn't mind and he rushed off leaving a piece of his trousers hanging there.

Soon he started to feel worried, and he decided to make straight for the railway station and catch the first train home. The station was no distance away so he started to walk.

Hardly had Boffin left the house before the owner and his little boy came back from taking the dog out for a walk. Now this was a bit of bad luck for Boffin, because the man was a policeman on his day off, and his dog was an Alsatian guard-dog called Carl.

As soon as they got in the boy went up to his room.

"Daddy, Daddy," he called out. "Someone's taken my piggy-bank."

His father and mother came running upstairs, and his mother told them about the man from the gas company. Then his father spotted the piece of Boffin's trousers still hanging on the nail.

"Here, boy," he called to the dog, "find him," and he held out the piece of trousers. Carl needed only one sniff, and then he was off down the road, pulling at his lead with his master behind him.

Boffin was by this time halfway to safety, but as he hurried along he suddenly heard a dog barking and he broke into a shambling trot. Sweat started to pour down his face.

"Mind where you're going, mate," protested a workman, as Boffin elbowed his way through the crowds.

By the time he reached the station Boffin was really frightened because he could now see the police-dog in the distance, working his way along, obviously on a hot scent. Boffin realized that he had three minutes before his train went and, grabbing his ticket, he rushed through the barrier to the platform where he could see the train waiting and the guard standing with the whistle at his lips.

"'Ere, wait for me!" he bellowed, and then, to his horror, he saw that all the carriages were packed to overflowing with cheering people hanging out of the windows. It was a Football Special! He could now hear close behind him a dog's eager panting.

Gasping and sweating he tore down the line of crowded carriages. No, it can't be – yes, it is. Safety at last for Boffin: the end carriage was completely empty.

He wrenched excitedly at the door handle. It was locked. The guard blew his whistle, and running footsteps and furious barking sounded now only a few feet away. Gasping for breath, Boffin pushed down the carriage window, threw in his bag and dived in.

"Done it, by gum!" He gasped as the train gave a piercing whistle and started to move forward. Boffin stuck his head out of the window and made rude signs at the policeman. The dog was now barking and jumping at the carriage window.

"Not today, thank you," jeered Boffin, red-faced but grinning in triumph.

Then he suddenly felt that something was wrong, very wrong indeed. The train was certainly moving, but his carriage was standing still: yes, for a long time. It was due for repairs. That's why it was locked.

Boffin started to yell and howl with rage. The policeman and his dog stopped panting, and then they both began to smile. It was their turn to laugh now.

Paul Learns to Throw

It was a holiday and Paul was bored. All his friends had gone to the seaside or were staying indoors. Paul had been sent out to amuse himself while his parents finished wallpapering the sittingroom.

As he wandered down the street he became aware of odd snatches of music. It sounded like fairground music! Paul hurried, groping in his pocket to make sure he had some

money. He clutched the coins excitedly as he saw that it was indeed a fair. Strange that he hadn't known about it before.

All his favourite amusements were there, he noticed. There was one marvellous ride called "The Perilous Parachute" which was causing several of its girl passengers to shut their eyes and scream. Paul decided to try that first of all. He gazed up at the huge machine, waiting eagerly for it to stop. It slowed down, and the girls got off, giggling in relief. Paul clambered into one of the covered seats, and fixed the bar across the front. With a jarring and screeching of music, the "Perilous Parachute" whirled upwards, to dash down again towards the ground, then back up, above the whole fairground in its blaze of lights.

Then Paul wandered through the crowds to the dodgem cars. He was not a very good driver and the other cars bumped him much more often than he bumped them.

As he looked around, wondering what to do next, Paul heard the sharp "clack!" of wood against wood. The coconut-shie stood nearby. Paul paused. He was not very good at throwing. All his friends were better at knocking empty tins off walls with stones, or bowling at cricket than he was. They made fun of Paul for being such a poor shot.

"If I could win a coconut to take home," he thought, "that would show them."

A fat man was in charge of the coconut-shy, and an even fatter customer was hurling wooden balls at the coconuts perched on their stands. He had a good aim, and triumphantly brought down a coconut with his third ball. The showman's assistant, a young lad, collected the lost balls, and set up another coconut ready for the next customer. Paul handed over his last few coins, and was given six balls. He took careful aim, and threw. Not a single ball even grazed the hair of a coconut.

"Oh, why can't I throw properly!" he muttered to himself, and stood there, glumly, as the showman's helper gathered up the balls.

"Want another try?" asked the showman, seeing Paul still there.

"Got no money," replied Paul. "Besides, it's no good. I can't throw straight. I'm hopeless."

"Cheer up, now! It's not that difficult, you know. It's just the knack you need."

"Yes, it's simple really," added the assistant. "Watch me."

He picked up a ball, flicked his wrist, and there, like magic, lay a coconut on the ground. He did it again. Paul stared at him in amazement and envy.

"You couldn't teach me how to do that, could you?"

"What – give away trade secrets and have you win all our nuts!" cried the showman. "I should think not!"

The assistant looked at Paul, grinned, and whispered in his boss's ear. The showman frowned, then made up his mind.

"If you take over my lad's job while he goes off for his tea," he announced, "I'll teach you how to throw properly."

"Oh, thanks!" said Paul, eagerly.

It was hard work, running around collecting the balls, and quite risky, with customers tossing them in all directions. Paul was pleased to see that a lot of people were even worse throwers than he was. Three-quarters of an hour later came Paul's promised lesson.

"Now, hold the ball like this," said the showman, demonstrating. "And take a line on the coconut with your thumb – and fire!"

Paul watched, listened and threw. It was not easy at first, but gradually, he improved. At last, his great moment came – he knocked down a coconut!

"We'll stop there," said the showman, "before you take the lot!"

Paul picked up his precious coconut. He thanked the showman, thrilled. He had had a marvellous afternoon, and tomorrow, he could show his friends how to knock a whole row of cans off the wall!

Buried Treasure

Tommy and his sister Lucy were very lucky. For they lived in a house with a long, wide garden with lots of trees and bushes as well as flowers and plenty of space for playing in.

But there was one part of the garden where they couldn't play, even though nothing was planted there – this was a corner which had once been a rock garden, and where there were lots of big stones buried in the ground.

One day Father told them they could have this corner of the garden for their own. "You can do what you like there," he said.

But the trouble was that Tommy and Lucy couldn't make up their minds what they wanted to do.

"We could plant flowers," Lucy said, "or vegetables. Father is always saying how much he would like to grow vegetables."

"I know!" said Tommy. "Let's dig up all those big stones. Then we will be able to play there and maybe plant some flowers or vegetables as well."

So, very early next day the children started to dig up their garden. It was very difficult, for the stones were big and stuck deep in the ground. And besides, they were all tangled over with grass roots and weeds.

Still, Tommy and Lucy dug as hard as they could. Then Lucy found something made of metal.

"It's a box of treasure," she said.

"Bet it isn't," shouted Tommy. And he was right. It was only a rusty old biscuit tin.

Next, Tommy found something made of iron. "It's an old sword," he shouted.

" Course it isn't," cried Lucy. "It's just an old iron bar."

And this time *she* was right.

But a minute later she found a bone. "Oh dear, it must be a skeleton; look at this bone, Tommy!"

But it wasn't. It was just a bone a dog had buried.

All this time the children were busily

digging up the stones, of course. And at last there was only one left. This was the biggest one of the whole lot. They finally managed to get the garden fork right underneath it, and with a big heave and a roll and a bump they turned it over.

And that's when Tommy and Lucy got a big surprise. For underneath the stone were some worms . . . some pieces of broken pot . . . and some small flat round things!

Tommy and Lucy bent down and looked at them. Then they looked even closer.

It looked like money – it *was* money! "We've found treasure, we've found treasure!" they both shouted together. Then they rushed back to the house to fetch Mother and Father.

At first they wouldn't believe the children.

"Don't be silly dear," Mother said. "No one ever really finds treasure in their garden."

But in the end they came outside to see.

"They're right," said Father. "These are old coins."

Together they picked up all the coins they could find and took them back to the house, where Mother cleaned one with a little soap and some metal polish. Underneath all the dirt it was bright and shiny gold.

Later they took all the coins to a museum

to find out how old they were and if they were valuable.

Some of them really were gold like the one Mother had cleaned. Others were silver or copper. They were very old, too – someone long ago must have hidden them in the garden to keep them safe and then forgotten about them.

Father had all the coins cleaned very well and framed on some green cloth just like a picture. And after that, Tommy and Lucy dug a lot more in the garden to see if they could find more treasure – and Father, too, (although he pretended not to) dug a lot harder and deeper than he needed to when he was planting new flowers. But none of them ever found anything else.

Nor could Tommy and Lucy ever make up their minds what to plant in their corner of the garden. So they just let the grass grow and used it for playing games.

Grumbleseals Are Always Right

Boris was a brown bear who lived in Siberia. Every autumn he would eat lots of the small blueberries which lay on the ground, because he thought that if he ate enough of them he would turn into a piece of the sky and be able to fly. Boris didn't call them blueberries. He called them sky nails to himself and thought that when they disappeared in winter they were used behind the clouds for holding up bits of the sky. The birds laughed at him and nearly always got to the blueberries first.

"Rubbish!" shouted the birds when he told them they were sky nails. "These are just ordinary blueberries."

"Well, why can you fly and I can't?" said Boris. The birds all laughed and flew off in a flock together, having eaten all the blueberries.

"Go and ask the grumbleseals. They're always right!" they shouted as they went away.

But Boris had never heard of grumbleseals, so he went on eating blueberries.

One autumn the birds didn't come, and Boris had all the blueberries to himself. He ate and ate and ate until he couldn't eat any more. He stood on top of a small rock on the bank of the river, which was not yet frozen, and jumped. He landed in the river with a great splash.

"Obviously I haven't eaten enough of them," Boris said to himself, and he went back to spend the next few days eating before his next jump from the rock. This time he took a run at it and landed twenty feet out from the bank. In spite of flapping his paws very fast he had not managed to fly at all.

"Sky nails aren't doing the trick. I shall have to eat some more." Boris was now really quite fat and made a very big splash. He tried to fly every day. He got really good at jumping but never stayed up in the air for more than a second or so, and always fell into the river. He was determined to fly, and spent all autumn running and jumping off the same rock.

The days started to get colder and one day there was a thin coating of ice on the river. Boris caught a slight cold and so did not go

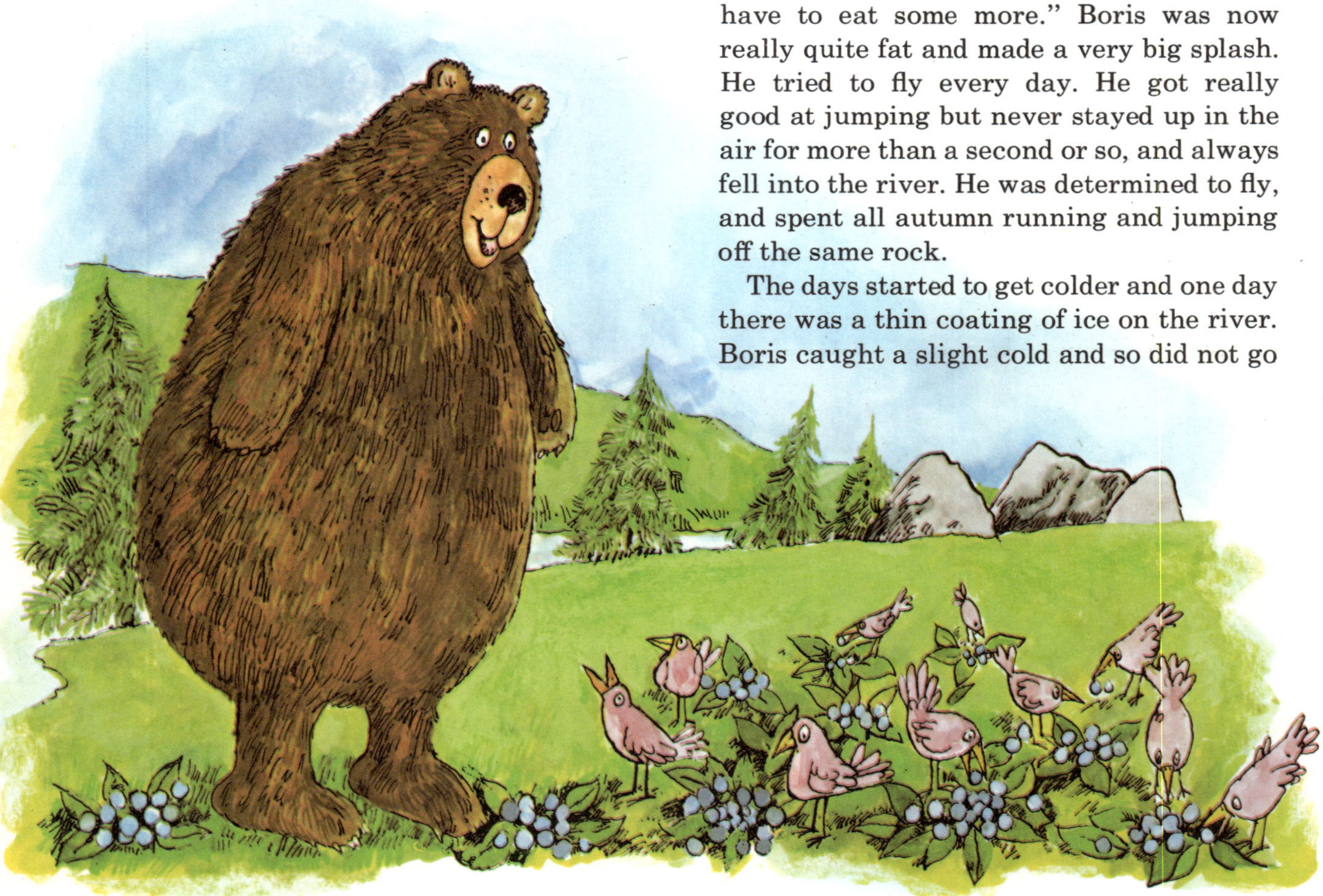

in the next day, and the day after that there was a thick mist and he found it difficult to see the river from the rock at all.

Boris took ten paces back, carefully measuring them, and jumped up and down at the end and flapped his arms. It had got very cold all of a sudden.

He ran and jumped into the air and started to flap his arms as usual. He couldn't see the river or the rock or anything except the mist.

Boris landed with a terrible bang on the ice. The river had completely iced over. He slid forward at great speed. The river was the same colour as the mist and, apart from the pain where he had landed, Boris might well have been flying. He kept flapping his arms as he slid along without a sound. The blueberries had not made him fly, but they had made him a heavy bear so that he slid along the ice for miles and miles. After some time he bumped into a large grey thing sitting on the ice. Then another, then another. They were grumbleseals, digging holes in the ice so that they could fish, but Boris didn't know that.

"Out of the way you big grey birds. Boris the bear is flying."

"BUZZ OFF! YOU ARE FRIGHTENING THE FISH AND BESIDES WE ARE NOT BIRDS BUT GRUMBLESEALS," all the seals shouted in chorus. They always talked that way, even to each other – never less than three in chorus.

"No, no, you're wrong! I'm *flying*!" said Boris as he whizzed past more grumbleseals.

"YOU WILL FALL INTO ONE OF OUR HOLES SOON IF YOU DON'T STOP," the grumbleseals said.

"Nonesense," said Boris and fell into a hole which a grumbleseal was fishing in. Boris spluttered and was helped out of the hole by two other grumbleseals.

"How did that happen?" Boris said. "I was flying. Someone shot me down."

"YOU WERE NOT FLYING. YOU ARE A FAT BEAR WHO WILL NEVER FLY, EVEN IF YOU EAT ALL THE BLUEBERRIES IN THE WORLD. BIRDS ARE DIFFERENT." Boris looked at himself and, walking back, had to admit that as usual the grumbleseals were right.

The Homing Pigeon

Walter sprang into the air and flapped his wings very hard. Faster and faster he flew – for he was a racing pigeon and he was practising for a very important race.

Walter lived with a lot of other pigeons in a special pigeon house on a small farm. The farm was in a wood between three hills; and it was called Three Hills Farm. Some days before, Walter's owner had put him in a basket and brought him to a place he had never seen before.

But now he was racing back home as fast as he could. He didn't have to be told the way, because, like all racing pigeons, Walter could remember the way home no matter how far away he had been taken.

On and on he flew. At last he thought to himself, "I'm nearly home – I can feel it in my bones! Any minute now and I'll see the three hills, the wood, and the farm."

But Walter was wrong. For though he flew on and on he never saw the hills. Or the wood. Or the farm. In fact, he saw nothing he recognized at all.

"I can't believe it," he thought. "I just can't have lost my way. The farm must be around here somewhere!"

So he flew in a wide circle. Then a wider circle still. But it made no difference. He was completely lost.

"I know," he thought. "I'll ask the way."

So he landed in a farmyard and called to a chicken. "Hullo, do you know the way to Three Hills Farm, please?"

The chicken thought very hard and asked all the other chickens. But none of them knew.

Then Walter asked the sheep and the cows. But they didn't know either.

Sadly, Walter left the farm and started flying round again.

Then he saw another bird – a swift.

"Hullo there, Swift," Walter called. "Do you know the way to Three Hills Farm?"

The swift shook his head. "Never heard of it," he said. "But come with me and we'll ask my friend Swallow – he travels round such a lot he may be able to help."

Swallow *had* heard of it. "My friend Nightingale told me all about it yesterday," he said. "I don't know how to get there from

here, but Nightingale does. Let's all go and ask him."

And so the three birds flew together to find Nightingale.

"Of course! I'll take you there, Walter," Nightingale said. Come along!"

And off they all flew.

But now it began to get dark. Swift and Swallow felt very sleepy, but they carried on just the same. Nightingale was used to staying up late, of course. Walter didn't feel tired, but he *was* worried.

"I hope we won't miss it in the dark," he said.

"Leave everything to me," Nightingale replied. "I know the way."

Then the moon came out.

"Now then, Walter," Nightingale said, "See anything you recognize?"

Walter looked. And sure enough below him he saw the three hills, the wood, and Three Hills Farm. He was home!

The four birds flew in together and perched on the roof of the barn.

"Thank you for all your help, Nightingale," he said. "And you, too, Swift and Swallow. I don't know what I would have done without you."

"That's all right, my friend," Nightingale said. "It was a pleasure."

"Glad we could help," said Swift.

"It was nice to have met you," Swallow said. "I'm sure we could be great friends."

"Goodbye, then," Walter said.

"Goodbye, Goodbye . . ."

Then, with a soft flap of wings the three birds flew off.

Suddenly Walter felt very sad. He didn't care about getting home late, or even about being a racing pigeon at all. He just wanted to be with his friends.

He knew what he had to do. "Wait for me!" he shouted. And he raced off after the other birds faster than he had ever raced in his life.

And so, as the moon rose high in the sky, Walter the pigeon, Swift, Swallow, and Nightingale flew back the way they had come.

Arthur Anteater's Cold

There was no doubt about it. Arthur Anteater had a cold. He had never had a cold before, and he was quite sure he never wanted to have one again. He had shivers up and down his back, his eyes were running, his voice was hoarse, and worst of all, his enormous snout was blocked all the way up.

"Yes, that's a cold all right," said Dr. Macaw, taking Arthur Anteater's pulse. "A stinker, I should say," he added, listening to Arthur Anteater's chest through his stethoscope.

"I should say so, too," croaked Arthur, gasping to get enough breath through his tiny mouth.

"Well, you must keep warm but get plenty of fresh air and plenty of good things to eat," said Dr. Macaw, snapping his bag shut. "Feed a cold, starve a fever. That's what I believe."

"But that's just the problem, Doctor," said Arthur. "I don't like to eat anything except ants, and every time I find a good nest I am just on the point of putting my tongue out to scoop up a mouthful when I feel a sneeze coming on. I try to stop it, but my nose is so long that once a sneeze starts coming it's like an express train and KER-SPLASH-OW, it explodes all over the place."

"Well," said Dr. Macaw, not quite understanding what Arthur was trying to say, "people usually do sneeze when they have colds."

"No, no, no," said Arthur impatiently. "When I sneeze over an anthill I blow the whole nest to pieces and scatter the little beasts out of sight. That's why I am extremely hungry. In fact," he added in a quavering voice, pulling the blanket up over his great long snout, "I think I need to be nursed, and have my ants brought to me on a tray in bed."

"Nonsense," snapped Dr. Macaw. "You're not going to lie there feeling sorry for yourself. In any case, if you were brought ants on a tray you would blow them all over the room just the same as you do outside. I'm going to make a telephone call."

Dr. Macaw flew across to the table where the telephone was, lifted the receiver and dialled a number.

"Hello," he said a few moments later. "I should like to speak to Mr. Michael Marmoset please. Oh, Michael, hello. Dr. Macaw here. I wonder if you could do something for Arthur Anteater. He will repay you with a large basket full of fruit."

Arthur Anteater made a protesting snuffle from under his blankets when he heard that, but Dr. Macaw silenced him with a steely stare.

"Good, Michael, I'm very glad to hear it," Dr. Macaw was saying into the telephone. "Now, I want you to go to the nearest store, buy three dozen of the largest handkerchiefs you can find, and I mean largest – Arthur has a sizeable nose, as you know – and meet the two of us under the big tree where I have my surgery in half an hour. See you then. Goodbye."

Half an hour later Dr. Macaw and Arthur, who was heavily wrapped in blankets, were standing under the tree waiting for Michael Marmoset to arrive.

"I don't know what all this is about," complained Arthur in a whimpery voice.

"You'll see in a minute," replied Dr. Macaw, and just then Michael Marmoset appeared, carrying a large brown package under his arm.

"I've got the hankies, Doctor," he squeaked.

"Excellent," said Dr. Macaw. "Here's what I want you to do," and he whispered in Michael's ear. Arthur just stood looking very gloomy, and wondering what was going on.

"Now, Arthur, cheer up," said Dr. Macaw. "I happen to know there is a particularly large ants' nest at the foot of this tree, brimming over with juicy, succulent ants. Just you start digging and don't worry about sneezing."

Arthur's eyes lit up at this, and he started digging furiously, quite forgetting about how he was feeling. Michael crouched beside him with one of the giant handkerchiefs. In a few moments Arthur had unearthed the nest, and there were thousands of ants swarming all over the ground.

"Oh, how delicious!" exclaimed Arthur. Then his nose started to wrinkle, and ATCHER-KER-SPLOSH! he sneezed – but right into the handkerchief which Michael had thrust in front of his nose, just in time.

"Oh, thank you, thank you," said Arthur, when he realized that they had stopped him sneezing the ants away. And he had a splendid meal. So did Michael Marmoset and Dr. Macaw, because Arthur gave them both a basket of fruit for their kindness.

King Kopplopplopploph

King Kopplopplopploph, whose name very few people could pronounce, lived on a small green island. Every day his subjects used to bring him twelve gallons of camel's milk, which he drank before getting out of his big, round bed. He was so fat that when he stood on one end of his small island the other end tipped up, and the tide washed round his feet.

The farms on the island had lots of camels, so nobody minded that he drank so much camel's milk. The rest of the people preferred cow's milk anyway, but they were worried that if the King went on drinking more camel's milk and getting fatter, he might sink the corner of the island where he took his walk. Cracks were appearing in the ground there already.

So, one morning, after the King had had breakfast and was sitting in his enormous bed, the people of the island went to see him.

"Oh, King! Oh, mighty and enormous King!" they said. "There are cracks in the ground where you take your walk in the morning, and the camels all think that it is an earthquake because of the tremors, and the plates fall off the racks in the kitchen, and the tiles fall off the roof."

King Kopplopplopploph had been asleep, but he woke up very quickly when he heard all the people in the room.

"Ah, a snack before breakfast!" He threw the quilt off the bed, and it covered the people completely.

"Where's the milk then?"

"Oh, King!" they said, rather muffled by the quilt, which was as big as a tennis

court. "It's after breakfast, and you have already had your camel's milk today."

"When people come into my room, there is only one reason, and that is to bring some camel's milk – just a little to help me face the morning." He took off the quilt and looked at the people. "You're not the ones who usually bring the milk, are you?"

"No, we are not," the people replied. "You have had your camel's milk for this morning already; and there is no more on the island, because the ground shakes too much and the camels are nervous and the milk churns fall over."

"I can't remember – but maybe you're right," the King reached an arm up and scratched his head. "Yes, now that you mention it, I *have* had breakfast. Well, if my name isn't . . ."

One of the King's favourite expressions was "if my name isn't Kopplopplopploph", but he usually had someone to remind him of it, as he had a bad memory.

He tried again: "If my name isn't . . . Anyone know it?" Kopplopplopploph looked round anxiously. "It must be there somewhere. I mean, we can't all have let it fall out of our heads . . ."

The people were so annoyed with the King that no one spoke – even though there were a few people who *could* pronounce his name.

"Your name is Fatso!" someone shouted.

The King was in a panic by now, and he believed that his name really was Fatso.

"What a terrible name! Oh, no!" He rushed out of the room, through the big doors of the castle and stood on the rocks on the other side of the island. The people who had come to complain followed him and apologized, but the King just stared out to sea.

He didn't move. The sun went down, and the sun came up again. The King was so large that he could sleep on his feet. On the third day, when the people had given up offering him bowls of milk, he started to get thinner, and thinner, and thinner. He got so thin that when he went back to the palace no one recognized him.

"Who are you?" they asked him.

"King . . ." He opened his mouth, but couldn't remember his name. Someone in the next room poured out some camel's milk. It sounded like SPLOTPLOPPLE.

"Kopplopplopploph!" he suddenly shouted. "And where's my breakfast?"

Mr. Pinktoe's Picture

Mr. Pinktoe was a businessman. He worked in a noisy, busy city. At the weekend, he cleaned his car and did odd jobs about the house.

One fine Saturday, Mr. Pinktoe was restless. He had worked particularly hard all that week and he felt that he needed a change. A day in the country – that was the answer. He would even take his old paints and easel, just in case he saw something which would make a good picture.

He headed for the country in his little black car, with a flask of tea, some sandwiches and his painting things on the back seat. Gradually the number of houses grew fewer and the spaces between them grew larger. Mr. Pinktoe wound down the window and took a good deep breath of fresh air. Hmmm. That was better than the dusty city.

He rolled slowly along, enjoying the scenery and looking out for a good place to have his sandwiches and do some painting. Soon he found the perfect spot, a field which sloped gently down to a small sparkling stream, with a herd of cows under an elm tree. He drew up, unpacked, and made his way across to it.

He decided to work before eating, so he settled in a shady spot under the elm and prepared his paints and easel. A picture of black and white cows, set against the blue sky and the green grass, would look very good on Mrs. Pinktoe's sitting-room wall.

Picking up his brush, he began. It was not easy to paint cows. They moved. They kept flicking their tails to keep off the flies. Mr. Pinktoe decided to leave out their tails and paint them in when he got home. But he did want to get their spots right. He tried following the moving cows around with his easel. It was no good. They were never still for long enough, and often disappeared altogether behind the tree. He had to get one

to keep still – but how? Then he remembered his sandwiches. Undoing the paper bag, he held out a tomato sandwich to the nearest cow. It mooed and came forward. It swallowed the sandwich in one bite, before Mr. Pinktoe even had time to pick up his brush. He would have to try putting the whole heap on the ground. That should give him more time. He would have no lunch, but he might get a good picture. So he laid the sandwiches on the grass, dashed back to his easel and held his brush ready. Unfortunately, all the cows saw the sandwiches at the same time, and the whole herd went after them. There was such a muddle that Mr. Pinktoe could not see one single cow clearly. To make matters worse, the sandwiches seemed to have made them thirsty, as all the cows started to wander down to the stream.

Sighing, Mr. Pinktoe picked up his gear and followed them. Unhappily, in the mud he missed his footing and slipped. Down he went with paints, easel and flask of tea. The cows raised their heads and stared as he struggled to his feet and set up his canvas again. His clothes were very dirty, but at least the cows were now still. But not for long. An aeroplane roared low overhead and, startled, they fled, leaving poor Mr. Pinktoe once again with his brush poised.

He decided to give up and go home. Just as he was leaving, it began to rain. Mr. Pinktoe ran for shelter under the elm, and poured himself a cup of tea. Then he noticed that all the cows were still – they were all lying down, as cows always do when it rains. Now was his chance.

So Mr. Pinktoe took home a picture after all. It wasn't quite as he had wanted it. The cows looked very small, all huddled together in the distance, and the sky wasn't very blue, but to make up for that, Mr. Pinktoe was able to paint a very beautiful rainbow.

George Gerbil's Visitor

George Gerbil scratched himself on the waistcoat front and stepped lightly down to breakfast. He was halfway through his breakfast egg when he felt a strange movement just behind the middle of his waistcoat. George Gerbil scratched himself again, and went back to eating his egg.

Two minutes later George Gerbil stopped eating. The itchy feeling behind his waistcoat was by no means gone. George Gerbil unbuttoned his waistcoat and looked inside.

"I don't know why it is," said a voice. "But I seem unable to spend a comfortable night."

"Oh," said George Gerbil. "And why would that be?" He had no idea why he was suddenly talking to someone. But he felt it only polite to reply. The voice seemed to come from somewhere on his person.

"Because people keep moving me around," replied the voice.

"Which people?"

"People like you. People in charge of things."

George Gerbil found that sort of remark hard to follow. He found it extra hard when a strange voice attacked him in the middle of his breakfast. It made him rather angry.

"Right," cried George Gerbil in a sudden temper. "We'll see about you, coming here without being asked first. We'll see about shaking you OFF!"

George Gerbil jumped up from his table and began to leap about. Briskly at first, then more and more fiercely. Gerbils are small animals, but their back legs are firm and strong; gerbils are very good at leaping about. George Gerbil jumped up and down for three minutes without stopping.

"I'm still here," said the voice from inside George Gerbil's waistcoat. "Why don't you give up and let me rest?"

George Gerbil shouted with rage and sprang into the top of the curtains. He swung there for a moment, jumped down to the

floor, and bounced halfway up the stairs. He leapt off the stairs to the top of the door. From the door he flew to the picture-rail, and then he performed a daring backward dive, tail-over-head onto the breakfast table. George Gerbil stood by the marmalade pot feeling out of breath.

"Very clever," snapped the voice from inside his waistcoat. "Now perhaps you'll kindly sit still for a few minutes."

George Gerbil scowled. "I know who you are," he suddenly cried. "I remember now. You're Harold the Phantom Visitor! You were over at the Bears' House last month. They told me you were most unpleasant."

"I'm a flea," said Harold the Phantom Visitor. "I'm a bit smaller than other animals, that's all. I need to look after myself. Find a bit of shelter to live in. That's all."

"I don't care," shouted George Gerbil. "You didn't ask if you could visit me. Now I'm going to get RID of you!"

By then George Gerbil was absolutely furious. His face was red and blotchy. He marched into his garden, climbed on his garden swing, and gave a great push with his strong back feet. It was dark in the garden, but George was quite used to riding his swing by moonlight. Gerbils are night animals, and start their day when it grows dark.

The garden swing rose higher and higher. Up and back swung George Gerbil. His evil temper had made him wild and ugly. Harold the Phantom Visitor clung on as best he could. Up and back went the swing. Higher and higher, the ropes creaking.

"This is your last chance," yelled George Gerbil to Harold. "Once and for all, will you get off me?"

"No," said Harold. "I won't."

"Yaaaaah!" shrieked George Gerbil, quite out of his mind. He gave one final thrust forward. The swing shot over the top and George and Harold were flung off the seat. High in the air they spun, round and round against the Moon, then down like two stones, one large and one small, plonk into George Gerbil's water-lily pond.

"Help!" called Harold the Phantom Visitor. "I'm off!" And he jumped away into the distance, leaving a tiny trail of water-drops behind him.

"Ugh!" cried George Gerbil. "How I hate the water." And he stood on a lily-pad on his great big feet, and shook himself dry.

"I wish I hadn't lost my temper," said George Gerbil. "Now my breakfast will be cold."

The Three Volcanoes

Once there were three smooth round hills – Big Hill, Middle Hill, and Little Hill. And though they looked ordinary they were really very special indeed.

For all three of them were volcanoes. Once they had breathed out smoke and fire and ash, and rock so hot that it had melted and become as runny as syrup. But that had been long, long before, and the hills had almost forgotten all about it.

Almost!

For one day Middle Hill said to Little Hill "I'm tired of Big Hill being bigger than I am. I want to be the biggest of the three of us. I want to be the biggest hill in the world!"

But Big Hill overheard him and didn't like the idea one bit.

"Oho, so you want to be bigger than I am, do you," he said. "And just how do you suppose you are going to do that?"

"By becoming a volcano again," said Middle Hill, getting angrier and angrier. "You thought I'd forgotten I was really a volcano, didn't you? Well I haven't, and I am going to grow and grow and grow."

And with that he began to breathe smoke and fire and ash.

Now, at first the other two hills thought Middle Hill was just being very silly. But as the days went by, all the ash breathed out by Middle Hill began to pile up, and he started to grow. And grow. And grow.

Little Hill still didn't care. But Big Hill became very angry.

"I don't like this at all," Big Hill said. "I mean, I've always been bigger than he is. It can't be right for him to start growing now – if I let him get bigger than me he might go on growing until he buries me."

"I'm sure he wouldn't!" said Little Hill. "He'll stop when he gets just a bit bigger."

"But I can't take that risk," said Big Hill. "No. Since Middle Hill has become a volcano again, I must, too."

And right away Big Hill himself began to breathe smoke and ash and to grow bigger.

As the weeks went by the two volcanoes went on getting bigger and bigger, and

angrier and angrier. Soon they were not only breathing smoke and fire and ash, they were also hurling great rocks into the air and pouring out hot liquid rock as runny as syrup. For miles around people had to leave their homes.

Little Hill was soon buried under all the ash and rock that the two bigger hills had thrown out. But he still tried to stop them.

"Please, please stop it – before something terrible happens!"

And sure enough, one day something really terrible did finally happen.

For the two volcanoes got so angry and so hot that they couldn't spit out all the fire and ash and liquid rock fast enough. And then, with a terrible long, rolling roar they both blew up!

The whole sky was filled with smoke and fire, and the ash covered the land for miles around.

When at last the smoke had cleared and the dust settled and people went to see what had happened, they saw that the two great volcanoes had completely disappeared. There were two burnt, rough places, where the two hills had once stood.

All that was left was Little Hill. For the force of the explosion had removed all the ash and rock that had buried him. He felt very sorry for what had happened, because all the people who lived nearby had had their houses burned and broken to pieces by Middle Hill and Big Hill.

So he tried to think of some way of helping everybody. Finally he had a good idea.

What was it? Well, he decided to become a volcano again himself! You see, some rivers flow underground, and there was one small river that ran right under Little Hill.

So Little Hill got himself nice and hot inside and heated this river up. That way all the villages nearby had lots of hot water. He even made a fountain which sprayed hot water into the air every hour.

In fact, since no one wanted to remember Big Hill and Middle Hill, they were soon forgotten. But Little Hill became famous all over the world.

Ernie Squirrel

Ernie Squirrel lived in a large walnut tree, just by the third branch from the top. He lived with his parents, Mr. and Mrs. Squirrel, his three brothers, Amos, Bertie and Caractacus, and his two sisters, Avis and Brenda.

Ernie was the youngest of the Squirrels.

One day when Ernie's brothers, Amos, Bertie and Caractacus, and his two sisters, Avis and Brenda, had gone to school, Mrs. Squirrel said to him:

"I must go to the shops today. You can play in the garden but don't go too far. And whatever you do, watch out for the Cat. Your brother Daniel didn't take care, and he finished up in the Cat's stew pot."

When his mother had gone, Ernie Squirrel climbed carefully, head first, down the walnut tree, clinging on tightly with all four feet. Soon he was down in the garden, hopping around the flower beds, exploring the vegetable garden behind the hedge. He stopped to look at a big red bucket, standing upside-down next to the turnips. A deep voice behind him said:

"You're a nice young squirrel."

Ernie Squirrel looked round. An enormous black cat arched its back and stared hard at Ernie. The Cat's two yellow eyes glittered. Its left ear was ragged and scarred.

Ernie said: "You're the Cat. I'm not allowed to speak to you. You ate my brother."

The Cat roared with laughter. "Ate him? No, no. Ate him? Ho, ho, ho. I didn't eat him. Just a little misunderstanding, that's all. Ho, ho, ho."

"Anyway," said Ernie, "You don't want to eat me. I'm too small."

"Oh really?" replied the Cat. He stretched out a paw and knocked Ernie flat on his back. The Cat looked at Ernie's tummy as he lay on the ground. "I don't know," said the Cat. "Maybe you are too small, maybe you aren't. Ho, ho, ho." And he shook with horrible laughter.

"Tell you what," said the Cat. "I'll let you go now if you tell me where you live. Ho, ho, ho. For later."

"All right," said Ernie Squirrel. "I'll tell you where I live if you can guess it in three guesses."

"It's a deal," said the Cat. "I love these games. Ho, ho, ho." He stared hard at Ernie. "First guess: the walnut tree, third branch from the top. A-ho, ho, ho. A-hee, hee, hee. I'm just wild about these games."

"No," said Ernie. "I don't live there."

"What!" roared the Cat. "All the squirrels live there."

"Not *all* the squirrels," said Ernie.

The Cat looked thoughtful. Maybe they didn't all live in the walnut tree.

"The oak tree?" guessed the Cat.

"No."

"The sycamore tree?"

"No. And that's your three guesses," said Ernie. "Now you must let me go."

"Oh, no," hissed the Cat. He lifted Ernie up by the neck. "You just tell me where you live, little squirrel. Or I'll eat you today!"

"Oh, dear," said Ernie. "All right. I live in that old willow tree by the stream." And he pointed to the far side of the garden.

The Cat looked surprised, but he let Ernie go.

Ernie Squirrel went home, and later he and the other squirrels made a plan.

That night the Cat crept towards the old willow tree by the stream. He looked slowly round in the dim light and saw a large squirrel sitting on the end of a branch. It was Amos Squirrel, Ernie's eldest brother.

The Cat was delighted. So it was true about the old willow tree. And that lovely plump squirrel looked so tasty!

"Hah!" shouted the Cat, unable to hold back any longer. "I'll start with you."

And he sprang along the branch towards Amos Squirrel. There was a loud crack. The branch broke off, just where the squirrels had nibbled through it that afternoon.

Amos Squirrel jumped to safety, but the Cat was taken completely by surprise. He fell, howling, into the stream and was never seen again.

Ship in a Storm

Toby and Penny looked over the rail of the ship at the lights of the port of Southampton coast getting fainter and fainter. They felt pleased, sad, and excited all at the same time. They were pleased because they were going home – to America. They were sad because they had enjoyed their holiday in England very much and were sorry to be leaving. And they were excited because, though they had been on an aeroplane when they flew from America to England, they had never been on a ship before.

Suddenly Toby shouted: "Look, Look! You can see HMS *Victory*!"

"You're dreaming, silly," said Penny. "We're miles away, and its too dark."

"No I'm not dreaming. Look over there!"

And Toby was right, for as the ship sailed towards the open sea it passed Portsmouth and the children could see the lights shining on the masts of Nelson's battleship.

The day before they had gone with their mother and father to visit the famous old ship. They had read all about the *Victory* and Nelson and the battle of Trafalgar at school, but seeing the ship itself, exactly as it had been on the day of the battle long ago, made it all seem much more real.

When they couldn't see the *Victory* any more, the children went to bed. The weather was fine and their cabin was very comfortable. But while they lay asleep, the wind began to blow very hard, and when Toby went on deck in the morning the ship was crashing through great high, white-topped waves. The wind howled, and thin clouds of spray were blowing over the deck.

There was a sailor on the deck. "Now then, young man," he said, "you should be below where it's dry having your breakfast."

"I only wanted to see what the storm was like," Toby said. "I'll go below now."

And so he did. Except that Penny wanted to see what the storm looked like, too.

Mother didn't want them to go on deck, but they could see very well through the big portholes in the room where they had breakfast.

Then, when they had nearly finished eating, they felt the great liner suddenly steer

hard to the right; at the same time the engines raced as the captain put them in reverse to stop the ship.

"Come on, Penny," Toby shouted. "I don't care what anyone says, I'm going up on deck to see what's the matter."

And off he ran, with Penny and Father and Mother close behind him.

When they got on deck they could hardly believe their eyes. For right in front of the big liner was another ship. But a ship looking like a picture in a book – looking a bit like Nelson's *Victory* in fact.

It was a sailing ship with rope ladders and three tall masts. Or rather two tall ones and one half-sized, because the middle mast had been broken in half by the storm.

Just then the sailor who had spoken to Toby passed by. "Hullo again," he said.

"Please, what's happening?" Penny asked. "Is that old sailing ship going to sink?"

"No, No. She'll be all right. *Now!* But its lucky we saw her when we did. She's what's called a sail training ship. Most of her crew are quite young boys learning how to be seamen."

"Why is she stopped like that," Father said. "Doesn't she have any engine at all?"

"Her engine broke down when she was hit by the wave that broke her mast," the sailor said. "They've only just got their radio working again, too – that's the reason we came so close to hitting her."

"What's going to happen now?" Toby asked.

"See for yourself," replied the sailor.

Slowly the big liner edged forward until she was shielding the training ship from the wind and the worst of the waves. The liner had radioed for more help, and later in the day a rescue tug arrived from England. A rope was fired across to the sailing ship. Then the tug took her in tow, back to port.

The liner and Toby and Penny then carried on towards America.

"Well, Penny," Toby said, "we saved our best adventure for last, didn't we?"

Augustus Gander

Augustus Gander had the wind up. In the forest clearing, outside his cottage, a pack of thin, mean, hungry wolves waited. It was nearly four o'clock in the afternoon. In an hour, when the light began to fail, they would attack.

Augustus Gander locked and bolted his door and his windows. But how long would locks and bolts last against a whole pack of fierce wolves? To cheer himself a little, Augustus Gander lit a fire in the hearth. He piled it high with logs – until it blazed brightly enough to stop a wolf from climbing down the chimney. But what good would that do if the wolves broke down the door or smashed the windows? Augustus Gander was in despair.

At half-past four the wolves set up a terrible howling just outside the cottage door.

"A-whoooooh Owwww-owwwww. A-whooooh Owwwwwwwww-owwwwwww. In half an hour, Mr. Gander, we're coming to get you. A-whooooooh Owwwwww-owwwww."

Then they all snapped their teeth together. It made a fearsome, gritty, grinding noise.

"Help!" said Augustus Gander. He said it to himself, because there was no one to help him. His friend the woodcutter lived five miles away in another part of the forest, and would never hear his cries.

"What shall I do?" Augustus Gander asked himself. "If I could get under the floorboards and hide perhaps they wouldn't find me. But that's no use. Wherever I go the wolves will just search until they do find me. They know I'm here from the chimney smoke."

As he paced up and down the floor, Augustus Gander noticed something attached to his feathers. There, on the left side. He looked closer and saw it was a zip-fastener.

"I've never seen that before," he said to himself. "How odd."

Augustus Gander took hold of the zipper and opened it. It must be some kind of pocket. Augustus poked a wing through the opening but could feel nothing.

"I know," he thought. "When the wolves break in, I'll put my head in here. Then I shan't have to see what they do to my nice cottage."

Augustus was pleased with that idea. He decided to practise putting his head in the pocket. He poked his beak into the opening and looked around.

It was black as a tunnel. Or a small cave. Augustus pushed his neck through the opening. "How strange," he said. "There seems to be so much room."

Soon the rest of Augustus Gander's body was following his head and neck. Finally, he gave a little skip and his two webbed feet also vanished through the zipper. Augustus found himself walking down a dark corridor. The walls were smooth and soft as velvet. There was no light but he kept moving forward.

Augustus Gander walked on and on, for what seemed like a quarter of a mile. Eventually, with a gentle bump, he reached the end. He looked up and saw a square slab of straw in the roof of the tunnel. He gave the straw a push and it lifted up into the open forest. Augustus climbed through the roof of the tunnel. When he was standing on firm ground, he looked this way and that. A few paces from him, through the trees, he saw the clearing where his cottage stood.

Augustus Gander could not resist a tremble. There, round his cottage, the wolves were preparing to attack. They, of

course, had no idea that their supper had escaped. As Augustus watched, the wolves gave a terrible howl and charged at the cottage. Quickly they smashed through the windows with their terrible teeth and claws. Soon they were all inside.

"When they find I'm not there, they'll start searching for me in the forest," thought Augustus Gander. "There's only one thing to do."

Slowly Augustus Gander crept towards the cottage. Treading softly on his broad webbed feet, he slipped into his shed next to the cottage. He brought out a tin of paraffin, and poured it over the cottage door. He lit the paraffin and ran back to the forest. In seconds the whole cottage went up in a rush and a roar of flame, and all the wolves were fried to small pieces inside.

"Thank goodness for that," said Augustus Gander. And he ran off to tell his friend the woodcutter.

Gregory

"Gregory," said his headmaster, "lacks charm."

Gregory stood in the middle of the carpet. It was hard to tell whether he was listening to a word of what was being said around him. Gregory looked at the wall and thought of other things.

Gregory's parents stood by the window.

His father said: "But he has done very well at Greek, Latin, Mathematics, History, English, French, Biology, Geography, Botany, Physics, Art and Chemistry."

"That," said the headmaster, "is so. But as a boy he lacks charm. Wouldn't you agree, Gregory?" he added.

Gregory said: "Don't know."

But Gregory knew very well. He also knew something that no one else did. He knew that, in fact, he was hardly a boy at all. He was changing into something else. Gregory was changing into a flamingo.

Under his school clothes great wings were beginning to form. His toes were growing longer and more pointed under his school socks.

"I have also noticed," said the headmaster, "that for a boy of his size Gregory is losing a lot of hair. At the front."

Gregory's nose was beginning to curve. Soon he would have a beak. Gregory was very excited about these changes. More than anything, he wanted to be a flamingo. Perhaps by the end of the week he would be one, and could fly south to live by one of the great rivers of India or East Africa.

When he returned home with his parents, Gregory went up to his room and looked at his new flamingo-self in the mirror. He stood on one leg, folded the other under his tummy and laid his head along his back. Very good. Soon he would be ready. Gregory decided to fly away early on Sunday morning. He had read a great many books about flamingos. He knew how to search for worms and insects and small shellfish. Gregory was sure he would not go hungry.

Sunday morning arrived at last. Sure enough, Gregory had turned into the complete flamingo. His legs were now extremely long and graceful. His three front toes were joined by a fine web. And his wings were broad and powerful.

Gregory was up before daylight. He left a note for his parents on the hall table. In it he explained how he had changed into a flamingo, and was going to live by one of the great rivers of India or East Africa.

Then he tiptoed through the front door, took his bicycle from the shed for the last time, and rode down to the river. Gregory had chosen to begin his great journey from a field next to the river, where there was plenty of room to spread his new wings. For his last bicycle ride Gregory wore a long raincoat. He did not want people to stare until he was ready for them.

Down at the field Gregory left the bicycle against a hedge, and dropped the raincoat over the crossbar.

This was the great moment. Gregory's superb rose-red body caught the first rays of the morning sun. He straightened his neck and marched stiff-legged to one end of the field. Then he turned. A harsh cry came from his beak. Gregory began to trot forward, and his magnificent wings now unfolded and slowly started to beat. Soon the trot became a gallop, the wings beat faster, his head and neck inclined further and further forward, until at last Gregory was in the air.

It was a beautiful take-off. Gregory swept forward at a smoothly rising angle to the ground. In his new colours of rose and red, the feathers black at the end of each wing, Gregory flew towards his new life. His graceful neck was fully out-stretched, his slender legs were fully extended behind.

"Goodbye," called Gregory to the rooftops of the town, in a raucous but faintly sorrowful voice. "I'm off to live by the great rivers of India and East Africa."

One of the people who saw Gregory leave that morning was his old headmaster. From his bedroom window he saw a rose-red bird soar past in the sky.

"My, my," said the headmaster. "A flamingo. Such a charming bird!"

Claud's Good Ideas

Long ago, in the time of knights and castles, lived a knight called Claud the Clumsy, who was very bad at fighting.

In May every year a great tournament was held outside the King's castle, and the law was that every knight had to go once every two years and enter at least two different contests. Of course, some knights, like Sir Allan the Bold, the worst-tempered knight in all the land, entered for everything. But Claud only went in for the safest things – like tree-climbing in full armour.

At least it was safe the way Claud did it. For while other knights tried to get to the top of the tree Claud just went as far as the first branch, then stopped.

But, one year, as Claud was doing this, he shook a bird's nest with two eggs in it from one of the top branches. It fell onto the head of the knight climbing the next tree.

This knight was none other than Sir Allan the Bold, who was so surprised that he fell off the tree and knocked himself completely out.

The other event Claud always entered was swimming the castle moat. Sir Allan entered that too, of course.

But when Sir Allan had reached the castle and was halfway back again, he swam SMACK into poor Claud – who hadn't even reached the castle yet.

"Now you've made me lose another race," spluttered Sir Allan. "I challenge you to a fight to the death!"

Now, because he was a knight, Claud couldn't refuse or even apologize, even though he wasn't any good at fighting.

On the other hand, he wasn't stupid. So he thought and thought of how to beat the mighty Sir Allan. And finally he had not one, but *five* good ideas!

The next day a great crowd gathered to see the fight – or rather to see Sir Allan chop poor Claud into little pieces. Sir Allan wore a glittering suit of armour; Claud wore no armour at all, but simply carried a tall, wide shield. That was the first of his good ideas.

Sir Allan carried a long sword and a great heavy battleaxe. Claud didn't seem to have any weapons at all.

CLANG! CRASH!! CLATTER!!! Sir Allan's sword smashed into Claud's shield, again and again. But Claud wasn't hurt.

With a roar of fury, Sir Allan threw down his sword and flung himself at Claud, pulled the shield out of his hands, and hurled it down. Then he swung a mighty blow at Claud with his battleaxe. Claud dodged easily – without armour he could move much faster than Sir Allan.

And that was the second of his good ideas. Then he produced the third: a coil of thin wire, loop after loop of it, which he simply threw at Sir Allan.

Sir Allan wasn't hurt by the wire at all, but he got completely tangled up in it.

It was time for the next of Claud's ideas. A lasso. He just dropped the open loop part on the ground, waited for Sir Allan to step into it, then pulled hard.

Sir Allan hit the ground with a crash!

But he still wasn't ready to give up. So Claud used the last of his good ideas – a bottle of the runniest glue and a bag of the fluffiest feathers. He emptied both over Sir Allan's head.

In a moment Sir Allan's helmet was stuck all over with glue and feathers. He couldn't see anything at all, and he could hardly breathe. And the more he tried to scrape the feathers off the more sticky and feathery he got. He was beaten!

As a prize the king promised to grant Claud any request.

"In that case, Your Majesty," Claud said, "I ask to be excused from ever coming to the tournament again."

So Claud the Clumsy won and Sir Allan the Bold lost, their only battle. In fact Sir Allan was so ashamed that from then on the only contests he ever entered were tree-climbing in full armour and swimming the castle moat!

Nomo's Hat

Nomo was a gnome who lived in Boskey Wood. Every morning he used to take a long walk through the wood, seeing what he could find, because his favourite hobby was picking things up. Sometimes he found things to eat, such as nuts or wild strawberries. At other times he lit upon little odds and ends which he took home in case they came in handy. The trouble was, that his gnome suit had no pockets, so he had to carry everything he found under his hat.

Nomo was very proud of his hat. It had been made especially for him by a fairy hatter, who had long ago moved away from the district. Nomo's was the only gnome hat which had a red and silver bobble on the top, and a patterned red and silver trimming to match. All the other gnomes had just plain green hats, and were rather envious of Nomo.

One chilly morning, Nomo set off for his walk, with his hat pulled down low over his bushy eyebrows. He sauntered along, his keen eyes fixed on the ground, searching for anything which might have been dropped or lost. But it was not a lucky day for him. He walked for a long time without finding anything.

Then, suddenly, he saw something glinting in the grass. He knelt down to pick it up – it was a safety pin. This was certainly a very useful treasure to put under his hat. He raised his hand to pull off his hat – but all he seized was thin air. His hat, his special, unique, gnome hat, was not on his head! Frantically, he searched all around in the grass and undergrowth – no sign of his hat. He ran back through Boskey Wood all the way he had come, but still he could not see it. He searched until it was too dark to see, but his hat had vanished.

At first light next day, Nomo was hunting for his hat again. His gnome neighbours were used to seeing him poking about, and didn't think it was strange – until they noticed that he was bareheaded. They promised him that they would keep their eyes open for the hat, and Nomo, in desperation, promised in return that whoever found it could borrow it at any time.

He stumbled upon Brock the badger, asleep in his den.

"I say, Brock, when you're out snuffling around in the undergrowth, keep a look out for my hat, will you?" begged Nomo.

The badger agreed, and promised to ask his friends to look, too.

Nomo went on until he came to the stream. A minnow poked his nose out of the water.

"I say, Minnie, when you're swimming about in the water, keep a look out for my hat, will you?" asked Nomo.

The minnow agreed, and promised to ask his friends to look, too.

Nomo rather hoped that the minnow would not find his hat, because if it were in the water, it would no doubt be quite spoiled. Still, even a bedraggled hat would be better than no hat at all, for while he had been searching for the hat he had come across several things which he would have liked to take home, but now he had nowhere to carry them.

He caught sight of a squirrel scampering along the ground.

"I say, when you're running along the branches, keep a look out for my hat, will you?" begged Nomo. "It's got a red and silver bobble on the top."

The squirrel scratched his head. "Oh, I know where that is," he said, casually.

"You do?" cried Nomo. "Where is it?"

"It's in that oak tree over there," the squirrel replied. "Bushytail has it."

Nomo rushed to the oak tree. Sure enough, dangling from a knotty branch, there was his hat, upsidedown. He stared up, open-mouthed, as another squirrel ran along the branch and dropped a nut into the hat.

"What on earth are you doing!" spluttered Nomo. "That's my special hat!"

"Oh, dear!" said Bushytail, peering down. "I rather fancied it for storing my nuts in this winter, instead of having to go and dig them out of the hard ground."

"Well, you can't have it, I'm afraid," said Nomo, not so cross now that he knew his hat was safe. The squirrel looked very upset at having to give up his new store-room.

"I'll tell you what," suggested Nomo. "You give me back my hat, and I'll take you home with me. Among all the things I've picked up, there's sure to be something you can use to store your nuts in."

So Nomo went home with his hat on, and gave the squirrel a fine cardboard box.

How to Keep Cool in the Jungle

Walter Warthog was feeling hot.

"It's high time somebody invented a decent sunshade," he said, and flopped down on the ground in a cloud of dust.

"Why don't you come in under the trees and get cool?" said a deep, purry voice. "It's very restful here."

Walter Warthog didn't wait to reply. He could recognize the silky tones of that wily Leopard anywhere, and with an angry snort he was up and running away across the plain, his tail straight up in the air, like a flagstick. Behind him the scornful laughter of Leopard rang out from the clump of trees.

"One day I'll catch you napping," shouted Leopard. "Ha ha ha! Just you wait. I'm much cleverer than you are. Ha ha ha!"

"I'm fed up with that Leopard," said Walter when he rejoined his family at their drinking place. "Every time I go off for a stroll on my own he turns up and makes fun of me from the bushes."

"Yes, yes, dear. Life's very unfair," said Mrs. Warthog.

"It certainly is," said Walter huffily. "There am I, boiling hot and unprotected from the sun, looking for food for the family . . ."

"Nonsense! We look for our own food!" interrupted all the little Warthogs.

"As I was saying," went on Walter snootily, "there am I, doing my job supporting the family, and much thanks I get for it I must say, and I can't nip into the bushes for a quiet nap because that beastly Leopard is lying in the undergrowth waiting to have me for supper."

"He wouldn't eat you. You're much too old and stringy," said one of Walter's daughters.

"Well, I wouldn't like to bet on it," said Walter. "Besides, I need to get cool in the middle of the day. It's not good for my heart to be standing out in the blazing sun all the time."

"Then you had better get yourself a sunshade," said Mrs. Warthog. "In fact, I will make you one at once. Boys, girls, run off and find me six large leaves."

The young Warthogs went snuffling off in search of suitable leaves for their father's sunshade, and soon they returned with an impressive collection. Mrs. Warthog grabbed Walter's tail and tied the leaves onto the end of it in a circle, so that when he held his tail up straight it looked exactly like an umbrella, and the leaves were so big that they formed a perfect sunshade for his back.

"Yes, well, humph," said Walter. "Yes, not too bad at all. Can't think why I never thought of it before. Simple, really." And he trotted out into the open to see how well it protected him. It really was very effective, keeping his back beautifully cool under the hottest sun. The only difficulty was that Walter had to hold his tail up straight all the time, instead of just when he was running, which is what warthogs usually do.

"Still," he said out loud to himself, "things might be a lot worse," and he settled down to a good snuffle through the grass for something to eat.

All of a sudden he felt something warm and soft rubbing against his back legs. Before he could turn round to see what it was a familiar voice sent a chill down his spine and made the hairs from the top of his head to the tip of his tail stand on end.

"How right you are, old chap," said the voice. "Things might be a lot worse – for me, at any rate. This is a much more comfortable spot than those spiky bushes, and I do congratulate you on your splendid sunshade. You're not as stupid as I thought." Leopard was curled up behind Walter's back legs, enjoying the shade cast by Walter's new invention, and chuckling with pleasure.

"W-W-What are you going to do?" stammered Walter. "If you eat me you won't be able to share my sunshade. Anyway, if I may say so, it's extremely annoying of you to do this, because I fixed up this sunshade just so that I could get away from you."

"Yes, yes, very tiresome of me," agreed Leopard. "But I'll make a bargain with you. I promise not to eat you if you get your missus to make me a sunshade too."

Naturally Walter agreed at once, and later that day Leopard had a handsome sunshade of leaves attached to his tail. And it wasn't long after that that most of the animals in the jungle decided that they too would like a sunshade from Mrs. Warthog. It became such a fashionable thing to wear that Walter set up a business sign over the bush where they lived. It read: "Mrs. Walter Warthog. Maker of Splendid Sunshades. Tailor-made for Tails."

The Little Forget-me-not

Mr. Root was a very keen gardener. He always worked very hard, digging and fertilizing in winter, sowing and planting in spring and summer, weeding and tidying in the autumn.

Mr. Root's one fault as a gardener was that he only liked red flowers. It was no use his wife saying how much she liked daffodils or lilies of the valley or Michaelmas daisies, or how attractive a golden-yellow forsythia would look growing over their front door. Mr. Root would only allow flowers of various shades of red.

Last summer Mr. Root made a special effort with the flowerbed below the wall. He had planted a beautiful new Margaret McGredy rose, to blend with the scarlet rambler which was trained on the trellis. Along the border grew geums, nasturtiums, salvias and poppies, all arranged according to height, and in neat rows, like soldiers on a parade ground. As a finishing touch, he stood pots of begonias and geraniums at equal distances on the top of the wall. Every morning Mr. Root would inspect his flowerbed to make sure that no garden pests were attacking his precious plants.

One morning, as he examined the bed, he had a nasty shock. There, in the blaze of scarlet and orange and red, was a single blue flower, an impudent forget-me-not. Mr. Root was flabbergasted. How had a forget-me-not, a blue forget-me-not, managed to make its way into this bed, creep up out of his earth, and produce a blue flower right under his nose?

"I'll have it up!" he declared, and stomped off to his shed to fetch a trowel.

The little forget-me-not shivered. "Oh, please help! Don't let him dig me up!" he pleaded to the tall scarlet poppies. They bent their heads down.

"Yes, we'll help. Plants must stand together." They spread their silky petals wider and wider, until the forget-me-not was quite hidden from view. When Mr. Root returned hot-foot with his trowel, he thought he must have been dreaming. He could not see the blue flower anywhere. He went indoors for a cup of tea to clear his head.

The forget-me-not knew that, though it had escaped this time, Mr. Root would still be suspicious. The poppies' short-lived petals would be dropping soon, and they would not be able to hide the little blue flower. The other plants put their heads together to think of a new plan. It was the rambler rose who provided one answer.

"When Mr. Root comes along tomorrow, I'll ask his dog Brownie to sit down in front of you. Brownie owes me a favour for not pricking his paw while he was burying a bone."

So the next day, Brownie positioned himself on the path near the forget-me-not and the blue flower escaped Mr. Root's keen eyes.

But then the forget-me-not had a very narrow escape indeed. Mr. Root came to weed his prize bed, and was bending low over the flowers. His busy hands moved nearer and nearer the forget-me-not. Another moment, and it would have been discovered. It was saved by Mrs. Root's morning coffee, which Mr. Root liked piping hot. Hurrying off, he decided to continue his weeding the next day.

All that night, the little forget-me-not shivered. It knew that Mr. Root would be back with his trowel. It hung down its tiny blue head in despair, and all its luckier red neighbours extended their leaves in sympathy.

Sure enough, next morning, Mr. Root came along with his basket and trowel. This time he spotted the forget-me-not at once.

"Aha! So I wasn't dreaming! Right, this time, you're coming up," and he sank his trowel into the earth. All the roses and border plants watched sadly, and the geraniums leaned over the edge of their pots to catch a last glimpse of their friend. The soil around the forget-me-not's roots shook and loosened, and it lay with its root exposed on top of the flowerbed. The gardener picked it up and made for his rubbish-heap.

Suddenly, there came a shout from over the wall.

"I say, Mr. Root – are you throwing that forget-me-not away?" It was Mr. Root's neighbour.

"Yes, I am. Why, do you want it? You're welcome to it – you know I don't like blue."

"Oh, thank you very much. It's just right for my herbaceous border."

So the little forget-me-not found a new and safe home on the other side of the wall, and it grew and flourished all that summer and for many seasons after.

Oliver Cod's Adventure

Oliver Cod's mother was being very firm.

"You're just like all the others, Oliver," she said, wagging her fin sternly at him. "Curiosity has killed more cod than cats, and you are as nosy as the rest of them. Always sniffing around those nets, just because you think there might be some tasty little tidbits to eat, same as your father did, and your uncles and fourteen of your brothers and sisters, and look what happened. They ended up fried in batter."

"But they'll never catch me," said Oliver Cod. "I'm much too quick for them."

"That's what they all said," said his mother. "Now, you just listen to me. I've thought of something that will make absolutely certain you don't end up as the cat's breakfast or somebody's supper, even if you do get trapped in those nets."

Mrs. Cod rummaged in a cupboard in the rock and produced a very strange looking object.

"What on earth, I mean, what in the watery world is that?" asked Oliver Cod.

"It's a bathing cap," said his mother. "I knitted it myself out of seaweed, and you are going to wear it."

"Me! Wear a bathing cap!" exclaimed Oliver Cod. "You've got to be joking."

"Now, don't take that silly attitude, young Oliver," said his mother. "It may be the saving of your life. If you get caught in the net and the fishermen pick you out with a bathing cap on your head, they will either think you are some kind of new sea monster and throw you back in the water out of sheer fright, or they will think you are very rare and precious and will put you in an aquarium. Then all the people will come and stare at you, which might be very boring, but at least you won't be inside their stomachs."

Oliver seemed quite impressed by what his mother had said. But then he thought of what he would look like in a bathing cap.

"All the other fish will poke fun at me," he complained.

"Well, you can pretend it's a captured diver's helmet or something," she said, "but I order you to wear it."

Reluctantly Oliver Cod allowed his mother to pull the bathing cap over his head and button the strap under his chin. It did look rather funny, and even his mother had to bite her lips hard to stop herself laughing.

Oliver felt very uncomfortable, and swam across to the sunken ship nearby to look at himself in the mirror in the captain's cabin. A shoal of cheeky little sprats squealed with laughter when they saw him coming, and they made whistling noises at him through the portholes. Oliver Cod felt very angry with his mother, and when he saw himself

in the mirror he tried to wrench the bathing cap off, he looked so ridiculous. But then he thought – no, I may look funny, but at least I look different, and now I shall be the most famous cod in the North Sea. And with that he zoomed off to see what excitement he could stir up. Very soon all the most desirable Miss Cods were clustering round him making cooing noises at his fancy hat.

"Where have you left your motorbike?" they asked and giggled uncontrollably.

"Ha, I don't need a motorbike," said Oliver haughtily. "I'm the fastest thing in the sea as it is," and to prove it he shot away towards the surface. Suddenly there was a whooshing sound and Oliver was being plucked from the sea in a huge net full of glistening, leaping silver fish.

"Help!" he cried, gasping for breath. But already a large red hand had grabbed him.

"By gum," said a voice. "Did you ever see anything like it, Bert, a fish with a bloomin' hat on!"

"No, Joe, can't say I did. Here, fellows, come and have a look at this." All the crew of the boat gathered round to inspect Oliver, and soon they were laughing so hard that they forgot to keep a tight hold on him. Oliver wriggled free, and with one mighty leap he was back in the sea.

A few moments later he was back home on the bottom of the sea, and being comforted by his mother.

"They didn't think I was a monster, Mother, and they didn't think I was rare and precious," he complained. "They just thought I was ridiculously funny."

"Well, you are very lucky, Oliver Cod," she said, "to have such a sensible mother."

Oliver felt very humble and grateful to his mother for her good sense. Of course, he didn't stay that way for long, and later that day he was boasting to all the girls how he was the only cod ever to escape from the hands of the fishermen. But then he was very big-headed, and only a big-headed cod can keep a bathing cap on.

Francis the Potter

Francis the potter was not pleased with himself. But then he hardly ever was. For Francis was probably the worst potter in the world. Though he tried very hard and practised day and night, it made no difference. His round pots still came out all uneven, his square ones still leaned to one side, his plates were all buckled, and he could never make any two cups come out the same size.

"Oh dear," he said, looking at his pots and shaking his head. "I don't know why I go on."

Nor did anyone else – for no one would ever buy anything Francis made.

But the other potters felt very sorry for him and let him work for them – mixing clay or the coloured glazes that they burned on to the pottery to make it shine with colour. Francis was quite happy doing this, but he wanted to make things himself.

So he decided to go away. "Maybe I can find someone who will teach me to make pots properly," he said.

He packed his bags and set out. He travelled many, many days until he came to a little town he had once been told about. In this town lived three famous potters.

"If one of these can't teach me to make pots, nobody can," he thought.

The first of the three famous potters made china figures of people, china bunches of flowers, china animals, china trains, and china motor cars. They were all beautifully coloured and very carefully made.

"Hmn, this won't do for me," Francis thought. "I can't even make simple things well, let alone difficult things like these."

So he passed on.

Outside the workshop of the second of the three famous potters there were all shapes and sizes of pots and bowls and plates and dishes and cups, all richly decorated, and made of china so fine that Francis could see the sunlight shining through it.

Francis went inside. "Could you teach me to make pots as good as these?" he asked the famous potter.

"I might," came the reply. It depends on

how good you are. Come, let's see what you can do."

And in the days which followed Francis tried his hardest to make the best pots he had ever made in his life and to learn what the potter told him.

But it was no good – Francis's pots still came out uneven and lopsided. Sadly he packed his bag again and went on his way.

There didn't seem any point in going to the third famous potter to try to learn anything from him. And so, when Francis came to his workshop he crossed to the other side of the road and walked quickly past.

But Francis hadn't gone far when he heard someone calling out behind him. It was the potter.

Francis could hardly believe his ears. "Don't go away," the potter called. "I've heard all about you. Come back to my workshop. Perhaps I can show you something to cheer you up."

This potter's shop was full of things with very simple shapes and glazes, though for all that Francis knew they were terribly difficult to make well.

"I can't make anything as good as that," Francis said.

"Come, come," said the potter. "Look around. Are you sure you can't see anything you think you could make?"

Francis looked again. Then he saw them! They were flat, and square, and all the same size – *tiles!*

"I never thought of tiles!" Francis cried. "I can make those well enough."

And right away Francis began thinking of lots of new patterns and colours for tiles. In fact he was so successful that the visitors who came to the little town that summer to see the work of the three famous potters bought as many of Francis's tiles as they could carry.

So Francis stopped being the world's worst potter and became famous as the world's *best* tile-maker.

The Two Dreams

Dick was crying himself to sleep. He was crying because his dog Timmie had now been lost for over a week. Timmie was a small white terrier with very shiny black eyes and a most inquisitive nose. He was eight years old, just the same age as his master. Until a week ago, he had come into Dick's bedroom early each morning when he was let out of the kitchen where he slept in his basket. Then he would jump onto Dick's bed and lick his face to wake him. Then he curled up on the bed and stayed there until Dick got up for breakfast. But a week ago, Timmie had gone off ratting and had not come back.

Dick's father and mother heard him crying from their room.

"It's no good," said his father. "I'll have to get him another dog." His mother did not reply, but she went to Dick and put her arms round him and talked to him until at last he fell asleep.

As he slept he had a strange and very vivid dream. He seemed to be standing on a fairly narrow stone bridge. He did not know what he was doing, but he felt it was something to do with Timmie. He just waited and waited, because he had a feeling that something important was going to happen. Then a little girl and a big man dressed like a farmer came walking across from the other side of the bridge, and as they came towards Dick the man pointed at him with his riding crop, and the little girl shouted and clapped her hands. They came quite close, and the big man smiled very cheerfully and bent down towards Dick. Dick didn't hear what he said, but when the dream faded he could see clearly the big man's cheerful red face, his leather gaiters and his riding crop.

Next day was market-day, and Dick drove into town with his father in silence because he was still puzzling over his dream. Dreams, he thought, were sometimes important: people saw things that we going to happen. His father stopped the car in the market square and got out to talk to some farmer friends.

Dick wandered away by himself, glad to get out of the market-day crowd. He walked on for some time, not noticing where he was going until he found himself walking down a twisty little lane that he did not recognize.

He was just going to turn back when he saw that it led out onto a bridge that crossed a canal. Yes, it was the bridge he had seen in his dream! He was so excited that his legs started to tremble, and when he reached it, all he could do was hold on to one of the steel rails and look towards the other end of the bridge.

Suddenly he heard a child call out "I *know* this is the place, Daddy, let's just have a quick look."

The two figures were just as Dick had seen them in his dream, and the little girl gave a triumphant cry: "There he is, Daddy, just as I said!" and she came running towards Dick, pulling her father after her.

Dick's heart almost stopped beating. Yes, it was the man, and he was smiling as he had smiled in the dream. He said, "My little girl here has some funny idea about you and a dream she's had. You don't happen to have lost your little dog, have you?" Dick nodded, unable to speak because of the lump in his throat.

"Well, we've got a dog in the car here. Found him in a rabbit snare a week ago. Proper messed up he was and half-starved. But he's all right now. We didn't know who he belonged to, and then last night my little girl here, she had this dream . . ."

Dick still could not speak, so he ran towards a waiting car where a frantic Timmie could be seen throwing himself against the windscreen. Eight days is a long time for a dog to lose his master, but it is nice to know that dreams do sometimes come true.

The Wonderful Flying Machine

Long ago, when aeroplanes had only just been invented and when they looked very different to aeroplanes today, there lived an inventor called Professor Sprogg.

Now it so happened that the town where the professor lived was going to have a big flying competition which Professor Sprogg was very, very anxious to win.

So he invented his own flying machine. For weeks he and his young assistant, Guy, worked on it – or rather Guy worked while the professor told him what to do.

At last, two days before the competition, it was finished. It had four big wings: two at the front, the others at the back. The engine was in the middle. It was made of wood, best cotton cloth, and string.

Proudly the professor painted its name in big red letters on its side – THE SPROGG FLYER.

But before the competition the Flyer had to be tested. So that same afternoon Guy attached it to the special launching catapult the professor had also invented, and then climbed into the pilot's seat. (The professor was really afraid to fly himself – he made Guy do it.)

"There's just one thing, Professor," Guy said, "I think it should . . ."

"Quiet!" shouted the professor. "Ready?"

Guy turned on the engine.

"Full power," shouted the professor. TWANG!! Guy and the flying machine shot high into the air.

"Hooray, it works," Professor Sprogg shouted. But he shouted too soon!

For no sooner had Guy got the Sprogg Special flying level than, with a loud crack, the whole thing folded in half in the middle and dropped straight into a haystack.

"I tried to tell you," Guy said, spitting hay, "It's too long and too heavy."

"Whatever can I do?" gasped Professor Sprogg. "We'll never be able to repair it in time for the competition now. I shouldn't have wasted my time. These flying machines will never work! Do what you like with the wreckage, I don't care."

And with that he walked gloomily away.

The day of the flying competition came.

In a big field just outside the town were lots of big tents. And inside each tent was a flying machine. The only empty tent – or so everyone thought – was Professor Sprogg's.

One after the other, strange-looking aeroplanes of every shape and size were wheeled out. Some had one wing; some had two. Or three. Some were shaped like bats, some like birds.

But in one thing they were all exactly alike. Not one could get off the ground!

"Well, that's the last," said the Mayor, who had come to present the prizes. "Nobody has won."

But at that moment, inside Professor Sprogg's tent, Guy finished his repairs.

"Wait a moment, Mr. Mayor," he shouted, running out of the tent and pushing his aeroplane in front of him. "It's my turn."

Professor Sprogg was standing in the crowd. He looked very hard at Guy's aeroplane. It seemed familiar.

No wonder! For it was no more than the back wings and engine of the Sprogg Flyer without the front, which had broken off.

"Silly idiot," laughed the professor.

But he stopped laughing soon enough! For Guy's flying machine had started to move. Faster and faster.

Suddenly it was flying! Higher and higher. Carefully Guy circled round and round. Then, as everyone held their breath, he landed. Perfectly.

"Hooray, Hooray!" the professor bellowed. "I've done it, I've won." And he rushed over to the judges' stand, where Guy was about to be given a big silver cup.

"What do you mean *you've* won?" asked Guy and the Mayor together. "Look–"

For Guy had painted over THE SPROGG FLYER on the side of his aeroplane. Instead, in big yellow letters, it said GUY–1.

The Clever Drummer and the Foolish King

Once there was a very rich but stupid king called Frederick and a very poor but clever drummer called Peter. Peter was a drummer in the King's orchestra. King Frederick didn't understand the first thing about music, but he liked to pretend he did, and was always having his orchestra give big concerts at the palace.

One day Peter had a wonderful idea for making himself rich. He went to the King's secretary and said:

"It's all very well for the King to have an orchestra and give concerts, but if he really knew such a lot about music he would find the best writer of music in the land to compose specially for him."

Well, the secretary thought this was a very good idea, and told the King. King Frederick was delighted, too (in fact he soon started to pretend he'd thought of the idea himself), and agreed to hold a music-writing contest.

Naturally he made himself the chief judge, but to help him he had the Queen, the Crown Prince, the Prime Minister, and his secretary.

Now, Peter wasn't really very good at writing music, but even so, he was sure he could win the contest. So he just signed his music with a made-up name and on the day of the contest sat with the other musicians.

Then the orchestra began to play. And play. And play.

The King listened to it all, and, of course, didn't understand any of it. Neither could any of the other judges – except one. The secretary. For at the end of every piece of music he looked across at Peter.

And at the end of every piece of music the drummer made an unhappy face and shook his head.

While this was going on the King was trying to think of something to write down about the music he had just heard.

"What did you think of it," he asked the Queen.

The Queen didn't know any more about it than the King; neither did any of the other judges, except the secretary – who remembered the way Peter the drummer had shaken his head. So he said:

"I didn't like it – not at all."

And so the king wrote "I didn't like it" on his piece of paper.

This went on all day until there was just one piece of music left: the piece written by Peter himself. This time, when the secretary looked at him, Peter smiled happily and clapped his hands.

So this time King Frederick wrote "I liked it" on his paper. And Peter won the competition.

After this, Peter went to live at the palace and soon became very rich – by writing simple little tunes. But then Frederick asked

him to write something special – something long and complicated – for a great concert on his birthday.

Poor Peter!

On the day of the concert the Royal Orchestra first of all played several pieces of music by famous composers – just to put everyone in the right mood. The king slept through most of this part of the concert, but the secretary quickly woke him up when Peter took his place in front of the orchestra.

But Peter was really very honest, and instead of beginning he said:

"Your Majesty. This music of mine is dreadful. I can't really compose at all. But there is some music I *do* want the orchestra to play. It's really a music lesson."

Then Peter got one trumpeter to play just one note, and then another note and another, until he was playing a simple tune.

Then he pointed to the clarinet-player, who joined in, and then he pointed to the violins, the oboes and all the other instruments, one at a time, until the whole orchestra was playing the simple tune. The King listened to every note.

By the time the orchestra had played the tune several times the King realized that he had actually listened to music for the first time in his life. And what's more – he understood it and liked it!

But the King had had more than a music lesson. For from that time on he always took the trouble to find out about things he didn't understand and never pretended he knew about things when he didn't.

And Peter? Well, he stopped writing music, of course. Instead he became the King's music secretary, his first job being to organize a music-writing contest.

A real one this time.

Lost Property

Fudge the bloodhound was very worried, and he wrinkled his forehead and shook his head sadly.

"Wherever did I bury that bone?" he asked himself. "I really must be losing my memory." Although Fudge was a bloodhound, he was only good at sniffing out particular things, like something tasty in the kitchen. When it came to finding old bones he was quite lost. He wandered vaguely from tree to tree, sniffing and sniffing.

"What on earth are you doing?" called out Sprock the squirrel from the tree above him. "Lost one of your old bones again?"

Fudge nodded his head gloomily.

"Now, look here," said Sprock, coming slithering down the tree, "you really must be more methodical."

Fudge nodded again.

"It's no good just nodding," the squirrel went on rather bossily, "because I don't believe you know what *methodical* means. It is being careful, remembering where you put things. What do you think would happen to me if I didn't know where I had put my nuts? Now, I have an idea for you: I will get a notebook and write down exactly where you put these bones of yours. Then, when you want one, you simply come and ask me, right?"

Fudge gladly agreed to Sprock's plan, and for the next few weeks the squirrel went with him whenever he buried a bone, and Sprock wrote down in his little green notebook the exact place of each one.

Then, one night, there was a terrible storm and all the trees in the wood swayed and groaned as the wind tugged at their roots. Suddenly there was a tremendous crack, and the squirrel's tree slowly heeled over and crashed to the ground.

"Don't panic, don't panic!" called Sprock as all his family tumbled out of bed chattering with anger and surprise. No one was hurt, and when the wind died down they began to collect up their scattered belongings and look out for another home.

By and by Fudge came along.

"Sorry to hear about your upset last night," he said. "No one hurt, I hope?"

"Oh we're all as right as rain," said Sprock airily. "We squirrels take this sort of thing in our stride."

Fudge coughed and looked even more worried than usual.

"Sorry to bother you, old boy, at such an awkward time, but I was just feeling that one of those bones would taste rather nice this morning."

"Of course, of course," said Sprock importantly. "Just let me get my book."

He paused and looked a little thoughtful. "Well, as a matter of fact, it happens to be in a rather difficult place at the moment because this tree that has fallen is blocking the entry. You could get at it with a lot of digging, of course, but then you're not much of a digger, are you? Oh dear, I'm sorry, what a bother."

Fudge then suddenly had an idea. "Wait a minute," he said, and off home he trotted.

There he found Tom the hunt terrier asleep in his basket. He thought of explaining to him what he wanted, but he decided that one loud bark was best. Tom sprang up quickly, his eyes bright and ears cocked. Fudge led the way back to the fallen tree where the squirrel was waiting, looking rather impatient. He began to explain to Tom where he ought to start digging, but the terrier waved him away.

"Leave this to me," he said, and, digging furiously, he began slowly to disappear from sight. Soon he could be heard underground, panting and yelping.

"I hope he knows what he is doing," said Sprock irritably. "Why does that rat keep popping up over there and making rude signs at us?"

There was suddenly a lot of scuffling, and Tom hurriedly backed out of the hole.

"Missed him by a couple of inches," he panted and disappeared once more. More yelps and scratchings were heard and then he appeared again. "Seen him?" he asked.

"I don't know what exactly you think you're doing," said the squirrel coldly. "We're not ratting."

"Not rattin'?" said Tom in a puzzled voice, "Then what are we doin'?"

"Looking for my green notebook."

"Why?"

"Because it tell us where Fudge has buried some bones."

"Then why didn't you say so at first?"

"We did, but you wouldn't listen."

"Some people," said Tom and the rest of his remark was lost as he disappeared once more down the hole.

There were a few more distant yelps, and the cheeky rat who had made rude signs appeared again the other side of the tree.

"You looking for something, matey?" he inquired, holding up a green notebook with an impudent grin. "You're just in time. I was taking it off to my old woman. She's always on at me about bedding for the new family." He tossed over the green notebook and darted down his hole again.

The Goggis

The Goggis stirred his soup in an old tin dish. He licked his lips and lifted the dish and slowly poured the hot soup into his mouth. When it had all gone, the Goggis reached up for his violin and played a soft and lonely-sounding tune. He became so carried away by the beautiful tune, so warmed by the hot soup, that the bow slipped from his fingers, the violin sank onto his chest, and the Goggis dropped off to sleep.

The Goggis was large and grey and hairy. He lived in a hedge near a small village. No one in the village quite knew where the Goggis came from: one day he wasn't there, the next day he was. But he told the most unusual stories about his life before he came to the village.

If someone asked him about a tune he was playing on the violin, he would wave his arms and say, "Oh, when I was conductor of the Batonberg State Orchestra, we played it all the time."

The Goggis lived a very simple life. If someone asked him about the old tin dish in which he ate all his meals, he would say, "Oh, it's a good old dish. When I was a colonel in the Hussars, we all used them. It's a regimental dish, you know. Special issue." Then he would tap the side of the dish with his fingers: Tap-tap-a-tap-tap. Tap-tap-a-tap.

The Goggis had a hat. It was mostly dark

green, with a black peak and black side-flaps, which he pulled down in winter to keep his ears warm. On top of the hat, in the middle, was a bright red button. If someone asked him about his hat, the Goggis would touch the bright red button on top and say: "Oh, I've had this hat since the time I walked to the South Pole." And how about the bright red button? "Oh, that's always been there. It saved my life once, you know."

Later in the day, while he was still sleeping, some children from the village came to see the Goggis. Sometimes he told them special stories, without even waiting to be asked.

Soon the Goggis woke up. He looked at the children, then he touched the bright red button on the top of his hat.

"Oh, yes," he said, as if someone had asked him about it. "That bright red button has always been there. It saved my life once, you know. I was riding through a pass high up in the mountains of Peru. In South America. When suddenly I was attacked by twenty wild Indians. Bullets were flying past my head. I stopped two bullets, by the way, on this old tin dish which was hanging round my neck at the time. I was unarmed, but I picked up some stones and scored direct hits on at least ten of the Indians. That scared them off for a while, and so I stepped behind a rock to think what to do next. There, behind the rock, was a huge poisonous snake. Straightaway, it wound itself round my legs. I was a prisoner. Just then an avalanche started. Rocks came roaring down from higher up the mountain. Terrible noise. Great rocks bouncing along the pass, squashing all the wild Indians that were left. There wasn't much I could do. Anyway, I took a firm grip on my violin bow and chopped off the head of the poisonous snake. That was him out of the way. Then I looked up. And there was an enormous boulder coming straight down on me. No time to move. I just stood there. It landed right on the top of my hat, hit this bright red button and split in two. The two halves of the boulder simply rolled away. Amazing really." The Goggis tapped the bright red button on the top of his hat. "Just a little red button. Saved my life."

"What happened after that?" asked one of the children.

But the Goggis was not listening. A few moments later, as the children still stared at him, he sank back in the hedge and went to sleep again.

The Secret of the Waterfall

Stephen stood on the riverbank and watched the waterfall come thundering down. He loved to come and stare at the waterfall because he thought it was such a fascinating and magical thing that it must be the guardian of some great secret.

Today, as he was staring at it, he noticed something different. There was a narrow ledge of rock running along behind the waterfall itself. When he went along the bank to inspect it more closely he saw that it was possible, if you were not enormously fat, to walk along the ledge and behind the great curtain of water.

He wondered if anyone had ever walked along there before. Perhaps they had, he thought, and were never heard of again. All the same, he couldn't resist the temptation, so, very carefully, making sure that he did not slip on the wet surface, he stepped out onto the ledge. Hugging the rock face, he inclined his way towards the middle.

The roaring of the water got closer and closer and the spray felt cold on his face and his hands. He did not like to look down below at the tumbling water and the glistening rocks way down at the bottom, so he concentrated on looking straight ahead. It was a very slow business, and he was a little frightened but he had gone too far now to turn back.

Suddenly he was behind the water, standing close up against the rock so that the water didn't catch hold of him and sweep him off the ledge. He was almost deafened by the continuous thunder of the waterfall. Only a little light was able to penetrate through the water, and Stephen had to feel his way along the ledge. It was very eerie.

All of a sudden the rock face ended, and he found himself falling for what seemed like ages into pitch darkness. He cried out in fright, but could not hear his voice against the waterfall. It seemed like a bad dream, going on and on falling, but, in fact, it only lasted for a second and his landing was not on jagged rocks, but on something beautifully soft. He had only tripped over the end of the rock face where it fell away from the waterfall onto a carpet of dead ferns and leaves and grasses.

Stephen sat up in bewilderment. Where was he? Far off in the distance a pale shaft of light shone down from outside. Then as his eyes became adjusted to the darkness, Stephen saw that he was in a cave, an enormous cave, and that on all sides he was surrounded by thousands of stalactites and stalagmites. The stalactites hung from the roof of the cave like long icicles, all sizes and shapes, and the stalagmites stuck up from the floor of the cave like huge, fat candles. Stephen noticed when he inspected them closely that they glowed in different colours – orange and yellow and pearly white.

"It is like a magician's cave," Stephen thought, "and it must be millions and millions of years old. I must explore it."

He stood up and searched around for a way through the stalagmites. Presently he found a path that led round the walls of the cave. Sometimes the path climbed quite steeply, at other times it twisted and turned, but everywhere that Stephen stopped to look, the view of the cave was different because the stalactites and stalagmites were in so many shapes and sizes. Sometimes they looked like organ pipes sticking up, sometimes like great sides of beef hanging in a butcher's shop.

In places there were tiny stagnant pools that must have been there for centuries, and once Stephen thought he heard the sound of a stream running close by. It was then that he realized he had walked so far into the cave that he could no longer hear the waterfall. The continuous dripping of the stalactites echoed coldly all round him.

Stephen started to shiver. It was chilly and wet in the heart of the cave, and he wondered if he could get out where the shaft of light was shining through. He hurried towards it, and when he was underneath it he saw that it was a trap door, with one of its planks broken loose. There were steps cut into the rock leading up to it, and Stephen scrambled up them and pushed the trap door up. He put his head out and looked around. To his astonishment, he realized that he was behind the hedge at the bottom of his own garden. He climbed out and rushed into the house.

When Stephen told his mother and father about the wonderful cave they didn't believe him. So Stephen decided he would keep the secret of the waterfall a secret.

The Enchanted Leaves

Once upon a time in a far-away land there grew a most unusual tree. It was special not because it was particularly big or small or very old or beautiful. Why then? It was unusual because of its leaves. All year round, long, pointed, glossy leaves hung from its branches, and these leaves were charmed. They had a strange magic power.

If a person had an enemy, he would creep into his house and hide one of these leaves under his bed. When his enemy went to bed, the leaf's magic made him sleep and sleep until the magic wore off.

This meant that some of the people were asleep for weeks on end, and didn't do any work. Sometimes there was no one awake to plant the seeds or build the houses or teach the children. Sometimes a whole family had leaves under its beds, and their home grew untidy and their animals strayed and their garden ran wild.

Now it happened that the old king of that country died, and his son, the prince, became king. This new king hated to see his kingdom in such a muddle just because of a tree, so the first thing he did when he came to the throne was to call his old teacher to him in private.

"What can I do about that horrid tree?" he asked his teacher. "The people are always picking the leaves and sending each other to sleep, so that my kingdom is in a great muddle."

"Well, your Majesty," replied the old man, "as long as the tree stands, the people will pluck its leaves. You must get rid of the tree."

"I cannot cut it down," cried the King. "The tree does not belong to me, and the people would be terribly angry."

"We must think of another plan, then," said his old teacher. "Let us sit quietly and consider the problem."

So the young king sat on his gilded throne with his head in his hands, and the old man sat on a wooden stool next to him, stroking his beard, and they both thought as hard as they could.

After a few minutes, the old man looked up.

"Really, it is not the whole tree which is causing the trouble, but only its leaves. We must pick all the leaves from the tree. Then the people will see that the tree has no further use, and it will be cut down."

"The perfect plan!" cried the King, and shook his old teacher's hand. "But we must

take the leaves secretly and gradually, or the people will notice us."

"We shall also have to hide the leaves away," said the teacher. "Wherever can we hide a great heap of leaves?"

"It will have to be a long way away from here," said the King, "so that nobody could find them before they grow old and withered and useless. Where is the furthest place that we know?"

He stared out of the palace window. He could see the enchanted tree in the distance, its leaves shining in the moonlight. The moon! That was the furthest place! The leaves must be sent to the moon. But how? Then he had an idea. He was the best archer in the land – he could shoot the leaves to the moon on his arrows.

So, late at night, the King would steal down to the magic tree with his bow and arrow, pluck a few leaves and shoot them on his arrows to the moon. He picked the leaves night after night until at last the tree stood bare. When the people saw that the branches were empty, they said that the tree was useless except for firewood, so they cut it down and chopped it into little pieces.

Now that no one could be put to sleep at the wrong time, the work got done, and now that quarrelling was not so easy, the people became friends. The leaves stayed on the moon, and their magic shimmered through its beams, so that at night, when the moon shone, everyone went to sleep – just as you are going to do now.

The Unwise Motorist

Maggie and Isobel Cow strolled along the lane towards their field. They had just been to the farm for milking. Behind them, in the distance, they heard the hum of an approaching car.

The lane was only a few feet wide, and much too narrow for two cars to pass each other. Every hundred yards or so, a special wide piece of road, called a passing bay, had been cut from the hedge. Any traffic on the road could then pass or overtake at these special places.

When Maggie and Isobel Cow first heard the noise of the car behind them, they decided to walk on to the next passing bay and there let the motorist overtake them. But the motorist must have been going fast, because suddenly he appeared at their backs. He honked his horn and shouted at Maggie and Isobel Cow in the most unfriendly way.

"Come on you cows! Get out of the way. HONK, HONK! Can't you see I'm in a hurry to get to town. Get a move on, you stupid, idle cows! Honk, honk!"

Maggie and Isobel Cow turned their heads to look at the motorist. They saw a large man sitting in a small red sports car. His face was red, the nose purple. The man wore a funny little pork-pie hat and a heavy sheepskin coat.

"Will you wait a few moments, please," said Maggie Cow politely to the motorist. "Till we come to the next passing place. It's just around the corner."

"You step aside, you cheeky fat cow," shouted the motorist. "I'm coming past now!"

And with a roar of his engine, the angry motorist moved forward and bumped straight into the back ends of Maggie and Isobel Cow. It gave them the most frightful shock.

"Moooooo!" they both called. "Moooooo! You mustn't do that."

"Bilge!" snarled the motorist with the purple nose. And he bumped them again.

"Moooooo!" called Maggie and Isobel Cow. Please don't do that again. It hurts."

Two large tears rolled from Maggie Cow's huge soft brown eyes. But the motorist took no notice at all. On came the small red sports car. Bump, into the back ends of Maggie and Isobel Cow.

"Right," said Isobel Cow to Maggie. "Watch this."

Isobel Cow had had enough. She edged herself backwards until she was almost touching the small red sports car. Then she kicked out with both back legs, and smashed the radiator grille and one of the headlights.

The motorist with the purple nose was so

surprised he didn't know what to do. Then Isobel Cow smashed the other headlight.

"Come on, Maggie," called Isobel Cow. "Now you have a go. Jump on his bonnet."

Maggie looked at the motorist with the purple nose who sat silent and trembling with fear in his battered sports car.

"No," said Maggie, "I think I'll jump on *him*. It's not the car's fault."

Then Maggie turned completely around between the fences in the narrow lane. She was surprisingly quick for a cow. In a second she had the motorist by the collar of his sheepskin coat. With her teeth she lifted him clear of the small red sports car and set him down in the road.

"Now," she said to the terrified motorist. "I'll give you ten seconds' start, then I'm going to chase you and bump you all the way to town. Mooooooo!" she added fiercely, full in his ear. "Ready. Steady. Go!"

The motorist rushed off at a great rate, his fat little legs hardly touching the ground, so frightened was he of the large, fierce cow.

"Moooooo," called Maggie after him, as he disappeared around the next corner in the road. She had wanted to scare him and she had done so. But she didn't want to chase him. That would be too much. Maggie and Isobel Cow heard the motorist's feet pattering away into the distance.

"Pity about his car," said Maggie Cow to Isobel, when the motorist had gone. "I'm not sure you should have smashed it up like that."

"No, perhaps not," said Isobel. "I lost my temper after what he did to our back ends. Still, made a lovely noise didn't it – those headlights crashing on the road!"

And Maggie and Isobel Cow mooed and grunted with pleasure at their victory over the Unwise Motorist.

Caroline the Cowboy

Caroline always looked forward to Saturday, when she played all the morning with her best friend, John. John lived next door. He went to school, so Saturday was the only time when they could enjoy a really long game.

Right after breakfast, Caroline told her mother, "I'm going to play with John."

"All right, dear," said her mother. "I'll call you when it's time for lunch. Mind you don't go outside the garden or trample on the flower beds."

Caroline ran across the lawn and crawled through the hole in the hedge. John's mother was hanging out the washing.

"Hello, Caroline. John's waiting for you indoors. He's got a surprise to show you."

Caroline pushed open the kitchen door excitedly. What could the surprise be?

Then she saw. John was wearing a beautiful Red Indian costume. The trousers were brown with fringes down the side of each leg, and he had a little jerkin to match. Best of all was the headdress, a mass of gaily-coloured feathers, hanging in a long tail right down his back.

"Oh John! Isn't that super!"

"My uncle sent it," said John. "I thought we could have a game of cowboys and Indians this morning. I'm just mending my bow and arrow."

"Oh yes, let's!" said Caroline, pleased. "I could be your squaw and sit in the wigwam and cook your dinner while you're hunting."

"No, you can't," answered John. "As there are only two of us, and I'm the Indian, you'll have to be the cowboy. I've never seen a girl cowboy, but perhaps you won't look too bad in my cowboy outfit."

"All right then," said Caroline, rather disappointed. "Anyway, cowboys always win."

"I don't think that's fair," said John. "And it's silly. The Indians couldn't really have lost every single fight. No, this time the Indians are going to beat the cowboys. Especially now I've mended my bow and arrow. Let's go and get my cowboy outfit."

The two children ran upstairs to John's bedroom. John pulled a big black cowboy hat and his gun and holster from his drawer.

Caroline tucked the gun in her belt and put on the hat. John pinned a sheriff's star on her dress. But even with the star and the hat and the gun, Caroline did not look very like a cowboy.

"It's your hair that's wrong," said John. "Cowboys don't have long blonde curls. Can't you tuck it up under your hat?"

Caroline tried, but not one single ringlet would stay up.

"It's no good," said John, crossly. "We'll just have to cut your curls off."

"Oh no!" cried Caroline. "Mummy would be terribly cross. And I like my hair long."

"If you want to play, you've got to do things properly," said John, firmly. "I'll only take off a little bit. Sit down here and I'll fetch the dressmaking scissors from downstairs."

Soon, a pile of silky golden curls lay on John's bedroom floor.

"That's more like a cowboy," said John. "Look in the mirror."

Caroline looked – and burst into tears. Her hair was a dreadful sight, long in some parts and short in others.

"Oh, John!" she sobbed. "I wish you hadn't cut it. Can't you stick my curls back on?"

"Of course not, silly," said John. "I like it anyway."

Just then, they heard John's mother coming upstairs. She pushed open the door and looked in.

"Oh my goodness! You've cut off Caroline's curls!"

I expect you can guess what Caroline's mother said. The children certainly didn't play cowboys and Indians that Saturday. Caroline had to spend the rest of the morning at the hairdressers, trying to put her hair right. John had to stay in his bedroom till lunchtime, and his mother locked his beautiful Indian suit away for the rest of the month.

The Two Buses

Mr. Theophrastus Shilling was a large fat man. He had a shiny bald head, and he lived in a small town by the side of a large lake.

Mr. Theophrastus Shilling was a bus owner. He owned two buses. One was a new Express bus called the Lakeside Flier. It had a long silver body and was very fast. The other bus was old and small and not so fast. It was called Bert.

One rainy morning in winter the Lakeside Flier would not start. He tried to start his engine but it only made a few whirring noises and stopped. The Lakeside Flier coughed.

"Oh dear," said the Lakeside Flier to Bert. "I think I've caught a cough in the engine."

"Well," said Bert slowly. "You do sound a bit wheezy."

Just then Mr. Theophrastus Shilling arrived.

"What's this," he said to the Lakeside Flier. "You should be out on the road. Let's have a look at you."

And he lifted up the bonnet of the Lakeside Flier and stuck his shiny bald head inside.

"Hah!" said Mr. Theophrastus Shilling. "You're all right. A bit damp around the plugs, that's all."

"I don't know," began the Lakeside Flier. "I feel a bit dodgy all over."

"Nonsense," said the Bald Bus Owner. "You'll be better in no time. Out you go now. You too, Bert."

Then the two buses started up and drove away to work. The Lakeside Flier turned to the left and Bert turned to the right and they went off round the lakeside in opposite directions.

Later in the day, Bert was chugging along on the other side of the lake. He went round a bend in the road and there he saw a sad sight. His friend the Lakeside Flier had broken down and was standing by the road.

It was still raining and the Lakeside Flier looked highly miserable.

"Dear me," said Bert. "I'll have to get you home."

"That would be kind," said the Lakeside Flier. And he gave a little cough.

Bert turned round in the road. Then one of the passengers fixed a piece of rope between the two buses. Someone else put a blanket over the Lakeside Flier's bonnet to keep him warm. And they set off together. The Lakeside Flier was a heavy bus and Bert had to work very hard to keep going.

Soon they came to a steep hill. Bert drove up the hill as fast as he could. But halfway up he stopped. He could go no further. The Lakeside Flier was too heavy.

So they backed down the hill and tried again. And again Bert could not reach the top.

"I don't know," thought Bert. "I can't leave the Lakeside Flier on his own. Not in this horrid rain."

Then one of his passengers stood up.

"Come on," said the Passenger. "We can't leave it all to Bert. Let's give him a push."

Fortunately everyone knew Bert and the Lakeside Flier. So they all climbed down into the road and started to push. Then all the passengers in the Lakeside Flier climbed down to help.

Bert put his engine into gear. The passengers pushed. And they moved ever so slowly up the hill. They reached halfway and all was well. They reached three-quarters of the way and Bert was beginning to tremble and shake.

"Push! Push!" shouted the First Passenger. And at last they scrambled over the top.

"Thank goodness for that," said Bert. The passengers climbed back on board. And off they went again.

The rain was still coming down, as they chugged along. They were almost home when they met Mr. Theophrastus Shilling. He had come to look for them on his bicycle. He was soaking wet and his bald head was more shiny than ever.

Bert stopped to pick up Mr. Theophrastus Shilling. He put his bicycle on the roof and sat down in the front of the bus. He was shivering all over.

"Dear me," said Mr. Theophrastus Shilling. "I think I'm a bit damp round the plugs. Let's all have a day off tomorrow! You, too, Bert. You're a hero today."

Then Bert drove them all back to the garage, and they all went straight to bed.

The Pig Quartet

It was autumn. Jennifer went to the country with her parents to stay for a few days on a large farm.

On the second day, after lunch, Jennifer slipped out of the farmhouse to explore by herself. She put on her coat and left the house by a side door.

Jennifer walked away from the farmhouse. She stepped round three puddles and went through a gate near the pigsty.

Just then she saw a line of pigs marching towards her. They looked very busy. There were four pigs altogether. Each pig wore a soft brown hat and a scarf around his neck. And each of them carried a black case of strange shape. The cases were narrow at one end, then they became gradually broader. Each case had a handle in the middle of one side.

The pigs looked very important in their soft brown hats. Jennifer stood by the wall.

The pigs walked briskly past her and climbed a path which led to a wood.

Jennifer decided to follow them. The pigs marched up to the top of the hill. Then they slid under a wire fence and entered the wood. Jennifer saw four pink pigs and four black cases of strange shape go into the trees. Soon they were out of sight. Jennifer crawled under the wire fence.

In the wood it was dark. The autumn ground was covered with leaves. There were red leaves and yellow leaves, and red and brown leaves and small twigs fallen from the trees. Jennifer hurried after the pigs. At last they stopped in a small clearing in the trees. Jennifer stood behind a tree and watched.

The four pigs opened their cases of strange shape. They brought out four small folding stools and set them up on the ground. Then they lifted from their cases the most beautiful violins Jennifer had ever seen. At least they looked like violins. But some were bigger than others. After a while Jennifer sorted them out to herself. There were two violins, and a viola and the largest one was a cello.

The four pigs sat down on their stools. Each pig held a string bow in one upper trotter. The pig with the cello looked sternly at the other pigs. He lifted his bow and said:

"Right lads. Number three."

And the pigs began to play. Two violins,

viola and cello. They began softly. Then their bows moved more sharply from side to side and the sound grew louder. As the sound became louder, a large red leaf lifted up from the ground and floated in the air. Two small yellow leaves rose into the air, then a huge floppy brown leaf drifted across the floor of the clearing and up in the air, waving here and there with the other leaves.

Soon the air in the clearing was filled with floating leaves. In the middle the four pigs sat on their folding stools and played their music.

After some minutes the music slowed down. It ended on one long low note. And the leaves floated down again to settle in their old places on the ground.

Jennifer was delighted. She clapped her hands together.

"Lovely! That was lovely!" she cried to the four pigs.

But the four pigs looked most alarmed. At once they grunted and packed up their black cases and made off through the trees at a steady run.

"Oh dear," said Jennifer. "Please stop a moment."

The pigs stopped and turned to Jennifer.

"Why?" they asked, together. They looked upset.

"Oh, I'm sorry," said Jennifer. "It was rude of me to follow you here. But I did so enjoy your music."

"Oh," said the pigs. "Did you?" They looked surprised.

"Yes," said Jennifer. "You make the most beautiful sounds I've ever heard."

"Oh," said the pigs. "Great. Sit down, will you." The pigs looked delighted, and danced about on the leaves.

Then the pig with the cello gave Jennifer his folding stool. They all unpacked their cases and played another beautiful tune. The leaves rose in the air once more and the pigs smiled at Jennifer. They stayed in the woods until it was time for tea. Then Jennifer invited them all back to the farmhouse for jelly and cakes and banana sandwiches.

Ginger Joe Meets Father Christmas

It was Christmas Eve, and the Barlow family was getting ready for bed. Jane and Timothy felt too excited to sleep. Their eyes were fixed on their stockings, dangling at the end of their beds. What would be in them when they woke up, after Father Christmas had come?

Ginger Joe, the marmalade cat, tucked his yellow head in his paws, and snuggled down into the cozy hearthrug in front of the fire. Close by stood the plate of bread and cheese which Timothy and Jane had left for Father Christmas's supper. Ginger Joe had strict instructions not to nibble at it, or he would get none of the Christmas turkey.

He slept, snoring slightly. Suddenly, he was awakened by a loud noise, and a bang on the back. The fireguard had tumbled on him – and there, sticking out of the chimney, was a large black boot, now dusty with soot.

"This is a tight one," grumbled an echoey voice, and with a last twist, Father Christmas emerged onto the hearthrug. Ginger Joe was amazed. Who was this bearded man, who had entered the room in such an extraordinary way? He watched, wide-eyed, as the stranger ate the bread and cheese with great appetite, then bent down to take several parcels out of his sack.

"Jane and Timothy Barlow," he said, checking the labels. "Right, upstairs I go. I hope their stockings are ready," and he crept out of the room.

Ginger Joe's sharp eyes had caught enticing glimpses of coloured and glittering ribbon in the huge sack which had been left on the rug. What was all this about, he wondered, and decided to examine things more closely. Wriggling out from under the fireguard, he wormed his way into the sack. What exciting shapes and smells!

All at once, he felt the sack being seized and hoisted up. Bumped and buffeted, Ginger Joe was carried up the chimney and out into the clear night sky where the reindeer were waiting with the sleigh.

"Gee up!" cried Father Christmas, placing his sack on the floor behind him. "We've got a lot to do tonight."

Ginger Joe, terrified by the unusual movement and his sudden removal from his cozy fireside, peeped cautiously out of the sack. He gave a loud mew of amazement. What was he doing here, in the night sky, higher than even the tallest tree he had ever climbed? The moon looked so huge, so close, and the snow-covered roofs gleamed far below.

Turning at the sound, Father Christmas could hardly believe his eyes. A cat in his sack!

"Whatever are you doing here? How did you get into my toysack?" he cried.

Ginger Joe explained how his curiosity had caused his present plight.

Father Christmas laughed.

"Well, my lad, I can't take you back, I'm afraid. Not yet, anyway. I'm Father Christmas, and I've all my rounds to do before dawn comes, and I can't disappoint the children on Christmas Day. You'll have to come with me, and I'll take you back when I've finished. I shan't be able to put you back in front of the fire. I'll just drop you off in a tree in your garden, if that's all right."

"Oh, yes!" said Ginger Joe. "I say, this is going to be fun."

So for the rest of the night, Ginger Joe went with Father Christmas. Up and down the chimneys, into the bedrooms where children lay asleep, across hearthrugs where other cats were curled up, and to whom Ginger Joe boasted about his adventure.

The sun was just beginning to lighten the sky as Ginger Joe and Father Christmas climbed out of their last chimney.

"It's Christmas Day, Ginger Joe," smiled Father Christmas. "Happy Christmas!"

"A happy Christmas to you, too!" cried Ginger Joe. "And thank you for giving me such a marvellous adventure."

"See you next year then!" said Father Christmas, as he drew his sleigh in close to the tallest tree in the Barlows' garden.

Ginger Joe scrambled down the tree, and watched Father Christmas's sleigh disappear into the sky until it was just a speck, then walked thoughtfully down the path. Indoors, Timothy and Jane were undoing their presents delightedly. Ginger Joe watched.

"Poor Ginger Joe," said Jane, hugging her new doll. "I've got a tin of sardines for him, but I don't suppose he can understand what's happening. Cats don't know about Father Christmas, do they?"

Ginger Joe just smiled to himself.

The Sea Otter and the Swimming Pool

James the Sea Otter lay on his back in the waters of a California bay and nibbled his lunch. It was a large and particularly delicious crab, and, like all sea otters, he ate it by balancing the crab upside-down on his chest and picking off the tasty bits with his paws.

"Ah, this is the life," said James to himself. "A sunny day, a calm sea, and quite the most excellent crab I've had for a long time. Even my young nephews aren't bothering me for once. All I need to complete my pleasure is a good book and a large cigar."

Of course, James had never actually read a book or smoked a cigar, but he had heard about such things from the gulls who flew over California and told him of the fat gentlemen who floated on their backs in swimming pools, smoking huge cigars and reading books. As James lay dozing on his back in the water, he tried to imagine what it would be like to swim in a swimming pool. All of a sudden he was awakened by the sound of an engine nearby. *Plam plam plam.* A big, grand-looking motor boat was bearing down on him at great speed. Before James could recover his wits and swim out of harm's way, he found himself struggling furiously in a very strong net. Then the net was pulled out of the water and James was swinging in mid-air, up, up, up, and over with a bump onto the boat's deck. He wriggled and barked and gnawed with his teeth and thrashed with his tail, but the net held him fast, and soon he flopped exhausted on his stomach. When he recovered his breath he realized that somebody was standing over him. James looked up and saw that it was undoubtedly just one of those men that his seagull friends had described. He was wearing only sandals, dark glasses and a pair of striped shorts, and he was so fat that his stomach flopped out over the top of his shorts. From his mouth protruded a large cigar.

"Hi," said the fat man without taking the cigar from his mouth. "My name is Hiram Gobblegook, and I'm just about the richest man in these here parts. I'm taking you home to my mansion, just so that I can be the only man in California with a sea otter in his swimming pool."

"What a coincidence," said James. "I was thinking about exactly that when you came along. But I must say, you were a bit rough in the way you manhandled me in that net."

"I wouldn't complain if I were you," said Mr. Gobblegook, "or you won't get any-

thing to eat. You won't find any crabs and such-like in a swimming pool, you know."

A few hours later, after a rather alarming journey by boat and then by car, James found himself in Mr. Gobblegook's pool. It was warm and blue and calm, and James was given a large rubber ball to play with.

"What fun this is," he thought, as he chased the ball up and down the pool, "and how funny those people are, sitting on the grass and rolling about with laughter at everything I do. I never knew I was so funny." The people threw him a crab, and he dived after it, and then ate it, as he always did, lying on his back in the water and using his chest as a dining-table. Everybody clapped and cheered.

"But what about a book and a fat cigar?" shouted James when he had finished eating. "That's what I came here for."

At this all the people clapped and cheered and laughed even louder. James thought this was rather strange, especially as Mr. Hiram Gobblegook was lying on a sort of inflated rubber mattress at the deep end of the pool, smoking a cigar and reading a book, and nobody was laughing at *him*.

"I'll show them," said James to himself. And with that he dived silently under the surface and swam towards the other end of the pool. He could see Mr. Gobblegook's mattress floating above him, and with one lunge he swam up and bit a hole in it.

PHOOSH! The air came whistling out of the mattress and Mr. Gobblegook started to shout and flap his arms as his huge, fat body began to sink with the mattress. Fortunately somebody threw in a lifebelt, and they pulled him out of the water.

"Throw that rascally otter back into the sea, where he belongs!" roared Mr. Gobblegook when he had recovered his composure.

Thus it was that a few minutes later James was being driven by Mr. Gobblegook's chauffeur, down to the sea.

"Don't you worry, James," said the chauffeur, as he pushed him out into the waves. "You're better off in the sea."

"Yes, perhaps I am," said James. "I know it's more exciting than a swimming pool, but I did want a taste of the luxury life."

"Ah, you don't know how lucky you are," said the chauffeur, and then they both waved goodbye, and James swam away very thoughtfully.

Stories by the six authors appear on the following pages: